A PRACTICAL GUIDE FOR OWNERS

# GOLDEN
# RETRIEVERS

A PRACTICAL GUIDE FOR OWNERS AND BREEDERS

# GOLDEN RETRIEVERS

ELANA ROSE

THE CROWOOD PRESS

First published in 2015 by
The Crowood Press Ltd
Ramsbury, Marlborough
Wiltshire SN8 2HR

**www.crowood.com**

**British Library Cataloguing-in-Publication Data**
A catalogue record for this book is available from the British Library.

ISBN 978 1 78500 037 9

Typeset by Jean Cussons Typesetting, Diss, Norfolk

Printed and bound in Malaysia by Times Offset (M) Sdn Bhd

# CONTENTS

# CHAPTER 1

# WHAT'S IN A NAME?

## A HISTORY

The Golden Retriever was originally bred, as the name implies, to retrieve, working mainly as a hunting companion to collect the game (originally waterfowl) that had been shot for sport. Being hardy, biddable in nature and soft in the mouth made the Golden Retriever an excellent choice for someone wanting a dog who would respond to commands, have a love for water and be gentle enough not to damage the game when retrieving it. Although the primary function of the Golden Retriever was as a hunting dog, over time, and as the breed gained popularity, it became a family companion and show dog.

The development of the Golden Retriever is attributed to Lord Tweedmouth from 1864 onwards, although the very starting point of the breed lies with a yellow, wavy-coated retriever bred by Lord Chichester. How the dog came into Lord Tweedmouth's hands is a matter for speculation. Perhaps he purchased him directly from Lord Chichester, but the more romantic version tells that he first came across the dog in Brighton, where

*Nous, the first Golden Retriever, photographed at Guisachan around 1870.*

he had been sold by Lord Chichester to a crafts-man; Lord Tweedmouth, impressed with the dog, offered to buy him. However this yellow retriever came into Lord Tweedmouth's life, one thing is for certain: both Lord Tweedmouth and the yellow retriever would set the foundations for the breed. The dog's name was Nous.

Nous was taken to Lord Tweedmouth's estate in Guisachan in Scotland, where he was mated to a Tweed Water Spaniel bitch called Belle; this breed is now extinct. She produced four puppies, named Crocus, Cowslip, Primrose and Ada. The bitches of this litter were outcrossed to different breeds, including an Irish Setter, another Tweed Water Spaniel and a Flat Coat Retriever. The bloodline produced dogs that were excellent workers, very biddable and handsome. Puppies were given to close friends, family and most notably Lord Tweedmouth's nephew, who would go on to breed Golden Retrievers himself. Nous's successors were bred true to type and became the forerunners of the breed we know today.

The breed did not, however, catch the public eye until Lewis ('Loulou') Harcourt, who owned a number of Nous's descendants, decided to enter them into a Kennel Club show in 1908 in the 'Any Variety Retriever' class, labelled as yellow Flat Coat Retrievers. They generated a great deal of interest, with many admirers wanting one of their own. Enthusiasts of the breed developed a breed club and breed standard, and campaigned to have the 'Golden' Retriever recognized as a different breed from the Flat Coat Retriever. Only in 1913 was the breed accepted by the Kennel Club. Glory for the Golden Retriever came in 1937 when Mr J. Eccles's dog FTCH Haulstone Larry won the Retriever

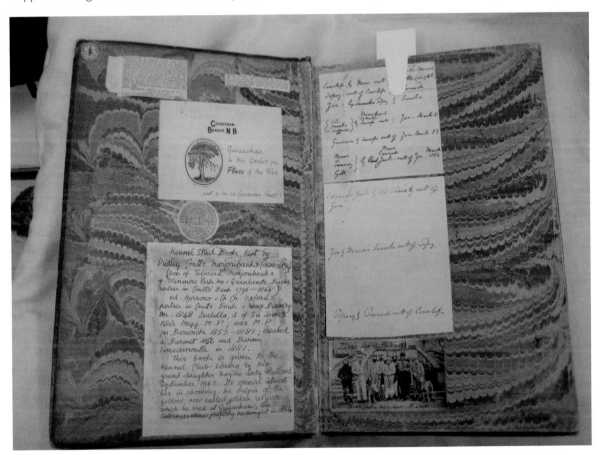

Lord Tweedmouth kept a record of matings, creating his own studbook.

Championship. From that moment onwards Golden Retrievers became an established breed, winning the hearts of many with their temperament, trainability and good looks. As the Golden Retriever's reputation spread, they became more appealing to people from all walks of life as a humble family pet, and thus they have become one of today's most popular dog breeds.

## BREED STANDARD

A Breed Standard comprises a set of guidelines describing the ideal characteristics, temperament and appearance of a breed, including the correct colour, and ensures that the breed is fit for function. Absolute soundness is essential. Breeders and judges should at all times be careful to avoid obvious conditions or exaggerations that would be detrimental in any way to the health, welfare or soundness of the breed. From time to time certain conditions or exaggerations may be considered to have the potential to affect dogs in some breeds adversely, and judges and breeders are requested to refer to the Breed Watch section of the Kennel Club website (http://www.the-kennel-club.org.uk/services/public/breeds/watch) for details of any current issues. If a feature or quality is desirable, it should only be present in the right measure. However, if a dog possesses a feature, characteristic or colour that is described as undesirable or highly undesirable, it is strongly recommended that it should not be rewarded in the show ring.

- General appearance: symmetrical, balanced, active, powerful, level mover; sound with kindly expression.
- Characteristics: biddable, intelligent and possessing natural working ability.
- Temperament: kindly, friendly and confident.
- Head and skull: balanced and well chiselled, skull broad without coarseness; well set on neck, muzzle powerful, wide and deep. Length of foreface approximately equals length from well defined stop to occiput. Nose preferably black.
- Eyes: dark brown, set well apart, dark rims.
- Ears: moderate size, set on approximate level with eyes.
- Mouth: jaws strong, with a perfect, regular and complete scissor bite, i.e. upper teeth closely overlapping lower teeth and set square to the jaws.
- Neck: good length, clean and muscular.

*The Golden Retriever.*

*Golden Retrievers love to be part of the family and join in with all activities.*

- Forequarters: forelegs straight with good bone, shoulders well laid back, long in blade with upper arm of equal length placing legs well under body. Elbows close fitting.
- Body: balanced, short-coupled, deep through heart. Ribs deep, well sprung. Level topline.
- Hindquarters: loin and legs strong and muscular, good second thighs, well bent stifles. Hocks well let down, straight when viewed from rear, turning neither in nor out. Cow-hocks highly undesirable.
- Feet: round and cat-like.
- Tail: set on and carried level with back, reaching to hocks, without curl at tip.
- Gait/movement: powerful with good drive. Straight and true in front and rear. Stride long and free with no sign of hackney action in front.
- Coat: flat or wavy with good feathering, dense water-resisting undercoat.

- Colour: any shade of gold or cream, neither red nor mahogany. A few white hairs permissible on chest only.
- Size: height at withers: dogs: 56–61cm (22–24in); bitches: 51–56cm (20–22in).
- Faults: any departure from the foregoing points should be considered a fault and the seriousness with which the fault should be regarded should be in exact proportion to its degree and its effect upon the health and welfare of the dog and on the dog's ability to perform its traditional work.
- Note: male animals should have two apparently normal testicles fully descended into the scrotum.

(© The Kennel Club Limited, reproduced with their permission)

## OTHER CHARACTERISTICS

The typical weight of a fully grown adult, in good physical condition, is between 25 and 32kg, with females at the lighter end of the scale. For a good indicator of the ideal weight, you should be able to feel but not see the dog's ribs.

As an active breed, being bred to hunt with the gun and retrieve game, Golden Retrievers are athletic, intelligent and confident, with lots of stamina come rain or shine. The close connection between dog and handler derives from the Golden's trustworthy and biddable nature; they have a sound temperament with humans and other animals, and are true all-rounders for all members of the family to enjoy.

## GOLDENS TODAY

The Golden Retriever's strong desire to work makes the breed perfect to train for a range of requirements, including hearing, seeing and handicap assistance, therapy, search and rescue, and other similar jobs. Goldens typically have a sweet nature and are happy to participate in mundane chores as well as adventures, as long as they are with their loved ones.

Dogs have an innate ability to touch our hearts, perhaps because of their unconditional love; few other animals appear to express emotion quite like a dog. A lick or a wag of the tail is very hard to resist, but match those qualities with a dog who can provide assistance and support, and you have a quite a friend.

What makes Golden Retrievers the ideal dog for such special jobs is down to some of these factors:

- they are willing to please and make good workers due to their biddable nature;
- their natural retrieving instinct makes their day-to-day jobs as assistance dogs enjoyable for them and they are easy to teach;
- being soft-mouthed means delicate jobs are more manageable for them;
- they have a calmness and loving nature about them, as well as a friendly appearance;
- they have a sound temperament; and
- they are the right size to be able to provide support comfortably to themselves.

Assistance dogs are sometimes bred specifically for their jobs by charities with breeding schemes, or they are donated by breeders or rescue centres, where personality fits type. As puppies, they should be alert, friendly, interested in things, confident and playful but not boisterous. They must, of course, also be fit and healthy.

*The Golden Retriever's appealing looks make them ideal service dogs.*

*Puppies have to attend classes to ensure their training is progressing to a level where they will be ready to begin service training.*

## DOGS FOR THE DISABLED

Golden Retrievers have been associated with the charity Dogs for the Disabled since its inception in 1988. Since then, more than 200 Golden Retrievers have been trained as assistance dogs for disabled adults and children, as well as for children with autism.

Like most other charities, Dogs for the Disabled sources puppies either through their own breeding scheme or from breeders. Puppies selected as potential working dogs go to live with volunteers, who socialize each puppy from the age of eight weeks and keep them until they are twelve to fourteen months old.

During this time they are taken everywhere and exposed to many situations to build up their confidence. They will be taken on a variety of transport types, into shops, into busy areas such as towns and cities, and in different environments. All of this socialization leads to a well-rounded dog; coupled with some level of basic training, it  provides the groundwork for an assistance dog. Volunteers are also asked to attend training classes and have monthly checks to see how each puppy is progressing.

At twelve to fourteen months old the puppies are returned to Dogs for the Disabled, where they begin training as assistance dogs. For the first two weeks the trainer will bond with the dog, a process that involves lots of playtime and cuddles. From there, the puppies progress into basic training: sit, lie down, stay, sit at a door and wait, recall, walk on the lead and settle. They are then encouraged to develop their natural retrieving instinct by fetching objects such as dumbbells. If they do not initially pick up the dumbbell, a treat is placed next to it to encourage them, and if they show interest in the correct object, a treat is thrown out for them. This develops into a clean pick-up, and is the same technique used in the field for training to collect shot game. The dog must also learn self-control and only retrieve when he is asked to do so.

Next the dogs are trained to pull objects by playing tug-of-war games with a toy, with rewards given to the dog when the object is pulled. The tug-of-war toy is then tied to things such as door handles to teach the dog how to open doors. Likewise, they are also trained to push. The process begins by teaching the dog to give his paw to the trainer, and then to place that paw on a mat. This mat is then moved around and the dog is asked to 'push' it. The mat can then be placed next to light switches or on doors. Gradually the mat's size is decreased until it can be taken away altogether when the dog responds on request to push an object. The lift exercise is taught in a similar way to the push, but instead of the paw the dog must touch objects with his nose. Other training includes being given a variety of objects of different textures to hold in their mouth without chewing.

Training becomes more advanced as the dogs are taken into more real-life situations, such as picking up socks instead of toys. Once this higher level of training has been completed, the dogs then undergo a qualification process, where they are assessed for ability and temperament.

Once they are fully trained, each dog is matched with his new owner. They are given time to bond with one another and to run through everything. An instructor will visit every week for the first few weeks, then every month, and then every six months to check that everyone is happy with the arrangement and the dog has settled in, and to provide support where needed.

The dog will go on to spend the majority of his adult life in his working role, until he retires. Owners, where possible, are given the option of keeping their dog and being provided with a new assistance dog, but where keeping two dogs is not suitable, the first dog will be rehomed either with a family member or with a friend, or as a last choice, rehomed with someone new.

Any dogs who do not achieve qualification, whether for health reasons or temperament, are normally kept as demonstration dogs and used to raise awareness for the charity. Most are often owned by staff.

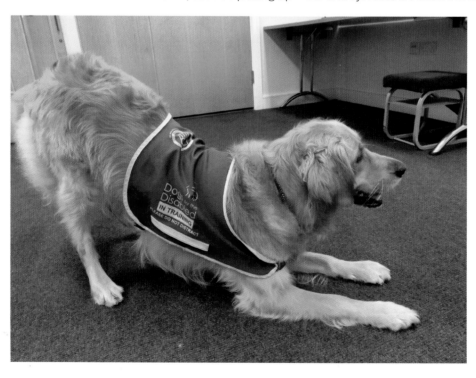

*Dogs in service training undergo numerous training challenges; the Golden's willingness to learn makes them a perfect choice for this work.*

A dog really can change a life, and it is no wonder that Golden Retrievers are the icon of such an important job.

## MEDICAL DETECTION DOGS

Dr Clair Guest, founder of Medical Detection Dogs, had first-hand experience of a sniffer dog detecting early signs of cancer with her own dog detecting the early stages of her breast cancer. Great research followed the discovery that dogs could sense abnormal/cancer cells through smells emitted by the skin, urine and breath. Dr Guest's first clinical trial was designed to prove that it was possible to train dogs to detect cancer in samples supplied by patients. Since then the accuracy of detection rates has risen, with a diagnostic accuracy for prostate cancer of 93 per cent. With cancers being notoriously difficult to detect in the early stages, utilizing a dog's incredible sense of smell is revolutionary. Dogs can detect odours at such low concentration because they have 300 million sensor receptors (compared to a human's 5 million). In 2012 the *European Respiratory Journal* published findings that dogs could detect lung cancer from only a breath sample.

Donations to the charity, along with trust funds, help to finance clinical trials in cancer diagnosis, working towards assisting scientists in the development of electronic systems (known as e-noses) that will assist in early, painless detection. The dogs provide screening for cancers that are currently very difficult to detect in their early stages. They all live with host families

*The Golden Retriever's sense of smell is forty times more powerful than a human's.*

and go to work at the charity headquarters; training involves sniffing urine samples, and the dogs are rewarded when they single out samples from known cancer patients from those of non-cancer patients. This level of skill requires a dog with a high working drive, who has a genuine love for working and natural ability.

## CANINE PARTNERS

Founded in 1990, Canine Partners works to improve the lives of those with disabilities by providing independence, which is often stolen away by a disabling disease. The independence comes in the form of a dog.

The dogs from Canine Partners provide day-to-day assistance with tasks that are otherwise difficult, painful or impossible to perform. They also provide special companionship and affection and can relieve loneliness by expanding social interaction, but most important perhaps is their ability to reduce their owner's reliance on other people.

These dogs, like those of most other such charities, begin their training with a puppy socializer, who teaches the puppy how to live within a household and achieve those all-important training hurdles, such as chewing, toilet training and sleeping through the night. They will be exposed to many situations and attend weekly training classes, as well as receiving checks by the charity, until they have reached maturity, when they are handed back to begin more serious training. The Golden Retriever is one of the most suitable breeds of dog for this job because of their natural ability to retrieve, their kind, biddable nature and their excellent working ability.

Once fully trained, dogs are matched with suitable owners and further training is tailor-made for each individual and their requirements, needs and abilities, thus bringing the maximum benefits for both dog and owner. The newly matched dog and owner are allowed time to bond with one another, allowing a relationship to form, for the dog to build trust in the owner and for the owner to develop pride in their dog, by learning about their character, traits and preferences.

Dogs trained by Canine Partners can assist those with even the most complex of disabilities, from all walks of life. There are now more than 300 active partnerships,* with the majority of those dogs being Golden Retrievers or Golden crosses.

   * Figure from September 2014.

### Canine Partners Case Study 1

*Jenny and Bliss: Jenny suffers with chronic back/pelvic pain and fibromyalgia*

'I have always had a zest for life but my condition over the years has challenged this side of my personality. Initially I trained as a nursery nurse, but unfortunately I developed epilepsy and moved job as I didn't want the children to see me ill. It was while I worked at the National Blood Service that I met and married my husband Daniel. From the start we knew we wanted a family of our own. Life was good until one day in April 2000 I collapsed in pain and was rushed for emergency surgery. It was here I was diagnosed with a twisted ovarian cyst.

*Canine Partners: Jenny and Bliss.*

'I collapsed again a year later; this time it was the other ovary that had developed a cyst. This time in surgery doctors discovered I had extensive scar tissue from my previous operation. Following this I suffered chronic pelvic pain, adhesion-related disorder, which then progressed into secondary fibromyalgia. As the months passed, the pain did not ease and many procedures followed, sadly to the point where I found difficulty in sitting and walking. Behind closed doors I felt under pressure and I fell into a deep depression. I just didn't want to be in the world and had a nervous breakdown that led to me trying to end my life. I was fighting a losing battle with my health and I lost my job and the home that went with it. I felt I had failed and had lost everything in my life that was "me". Losing my identity, role and place in life was the most difficult to handle as it also took my last bit of confidence with it. All I could see was a life ahead of pain, disability and being a drain on my family, especially my husband, who at this point had become my full-time carer.

'I then attended a specialist pain management programme where I learned to retrain my nerves and identify my values in life. Things started off well, but for a person who had always been the carer, I still found being cared for very difficult. I hated not being able to do the simple things like go out, do household tasks, shopping, get undressed on my own. I still felt I was a drain on my husband as he had to do everything for me, so I began not asking for things I wanted or needed to take the strain off him. I even relented to having carers come in to help with my personal care, which I hated; I felt I had lost my last bit of dignity but I just wanted to take that burden off Daniel.

'One day we attended a disability exhibition where we saw a sign for a demonstration for "Canine Partners". After the initial application, I knew there would be a long wait before I would be close to being invited along for assessment days, but boy I didn't realize how I would feel during that time. Every letter, phone call, my heart would skip a beat thinking, is this the day? When the call came that they had a match for me, I was over the moon but also a little nervous. But when the trainer pointed out this beautiful Golden Retriever, Bliss, who smothered me in kisses, her tail wagging furiously, it was that moment that I knew she was going to be my sunshine to brighten up my life. Two weeks before Christmas 2012, we started our life together.

'The first night she moved in I felt like a new mum checking on her to see if she was okay. The following morning I woke to the lovely sight of Bliss's face by mine as she wagged her tail furiously. It felt great that she seemed so happy to see me and excited to start the day, which made me feel eager to start the day too. I get this greeting every morning and it gives me that oomph, especially on bad days, to get up and start the day.

'Bliss and I have now been together for a while and it has been a life-changing time. For the first time in ten years I have hope, something I thought I had lost for ever. Bliss has given me a purpose in life again; she depends on me for all her needs and in return we have fun together whilst she works with me to give me back my independence. As time has gone by, Bliss and I have taken on new challenges and we are only at the beginning of our life together. I'm still amazed with the things she does for me and it always puts a smile on my face. It has not only changed my life but it has also improved my husband's life as he can relax more now we have Bliss.

'I love the little things – like, I can go to bed at a time I choose without having to wait for Daniel or to go when he goes, as Bliss helps me get changed, helps me into bed by lifting my legs up and then pulling the quilt over me before she settles herself down. It's not having to ask someone to pick things up for me or help me get my coat off. She has given me my dignity back as she helps me get dressed and undressed. We are always out and about on adventures as she gives me the strength to do things on my own that I haven't been able to do for a few years and it's an amazing feeling. I no longer feel trapped.

'She aids me in getting my lower half dressed by positioning my legs; she lifts and puts down the foot plates on my wheelchair; puts her toys away or things into baskets. She is trained to lift me up if I fall by bringing me a special item, then, while I hold onto it, she will pull me up from off the floor so I can be more comfortable. She also brings me the post; she loves paying the cashier when we go shopping and she gets the things off the shelves. She brings me the phone, remote control, etc., plus automatically picking things up if she sees me drop them.

'Unfortunately my condition has deteriorated recently and I now have episodes of unexpected painful spasms. After having them for a couple of weeks we noticed that Bliss would become fidgety at times, staring at me intensely, and what we have found is that she was doing this approximately twenty minutes before one of my spasm attacks; with this warning I am able to get myself settled, comfortable and importantly take my medication before it gets too bad. We don't know how she is sensing these attacks coming on but it is a huge benefit to me. The other area she has helped me with in a way that I never expected is by stimulating new nerves in my legs. She has done this by the way she lifts my legs. It is like the physiotherapy I was having for it but more intense as it is done many times during the day, thereby strengthening the message pathway and lessening the muscle weakness, which means I am now able to take a few steps, which is fabulous.

'Above all, Bliss has given me an unbreakable companionship that gives me the strength to carry on, even on the toughest days. Having a canine partner has changed my life in more ways than I ever expected. The physical help is just a small part of how she has improved my life; more than that is the mental and emotional support she gives to me that has brought out the happiness that I had lost and for that I am for ever thankful to Canine Partners for giving me Bliss.

'Having Bliss by my side gives me back the confidence that I had lost, and I know many of the days I wouldn't have gone out but Bliss gives me that motivation to get up and go. Even on my bad days she keeps me smiling and distracted from my pain as we play games together.

'And there is nothing better than a snuggle from a cuddly Goldie to make you feel happy. Bliss is the best present I have ever had.'

### Canine Partners Case Study 2

*Wendy and Edward: Wendy suffers with Dystrophic Epidermolysis Bullosa Recessive*

'I was born with the rare skin condition Dystrophic Epidermolysis Bullosa Recessive. My condition causes my skin to tear and blister at the slightest knock. My throat is also the size of a five pence piece and can close at any time, stopping me breathing. As my condition worsened, I found it difficult to open doors, use the cash machine, dress and undress. My husband

*Canine Partners: Wendy and Edward.*

and I also used to take it in turns to sleep each night, in case I stopped breathing.

'In 1993 my throat became so scarred and small that my husband Peter had to stop work to care for me. I hated hospitals and dreaded every appointment, shutting my ears to what they would say, and as a consequence my hands and throat became a nightmare to live with. Already painful, my hands were closing fast. I began to find it harder and harder to pick up or grip things and found it difficult to open doors and use locks. My oesophagus became scarred by acid, which came up every time I bent over to pick up things. My balance was bad; I had to hold on to Peter to walk and would not go out on my own at all. The pressure on Peter was tremendous as he was constantly on call, and cared for me without a break.

'I first met Golden Retriever Edward when he was just four weeks old. Because of my skin condition, Canine Partners felt it best I worked alongside one of their trainers with a puppy from the beginning. At nine weeks old Edward, who looked like a snowball on legs, came into my life. That very first night I had a sign language lesson at college and Edward came with me. He settled really well in class and was the most popular thing there at the break; college was never to be the same. Since then he has continuously watched our hand signs and I am now able to use these with him if my throat is very bad.

'When Edward was eighteen months old we attended a two-week residential training course with Canine

Partners. Fortunately we passed and it was wonderful to show the team at Canine Partners what we had all achieved and to take Edward home as a fully fledged assistance dog.

'Edward was to be the making of me. At last I did not worry about going to hospital any more. I am so wrapped up in him and his well-being I don't worry like I used to. The help he gives me is a bonus, and his companionship and his loyalty are the best thing about having him. He is always there for me. I have reduced my painkillers since having him. When the pain is very bad, I cuddle up to him or he gets a toy as if to say, "Come on, Mum, play and don't think about it." At home Edward helps me get out of bed, fetches my crutches and clothes, picks up anything I drop or need from the floor. He can open and close doors, load and unload the washing machine, get a warm towel off the radiator for after a shower, find named items, get my shopping off the shelf and then hand the purse to the cashier. He can also get help for me, undress me, balance me when I walk and generally comes everywhere with me.

'My husband is my carer, but now we have Edward it gives him valuable time off as I have got so much independence back. One night when Edward was about ten months old, my husband had fallen asleep and I stopped breathing; Edward immediately woke him up. Edward has proved to be so reliable at waking Peter that we can both go off to sleep knowing he will save my life.

'I am not allowed to cry as it closes my throat altogether and I have to go into hospital and be put on a drip until it opens again. Sometimes it is very hard not to get upset, so I just bury my face in Edward's fur and it all falls away. After all, nothing can be that bad as long as I have Edward. He even stays in hospital with me, as it would make my throat close if I got upset at being parted from him. The nurses have also found that he is the best one to undress me as he causes fewer traumas to my skin when he does it; no one is as gentle as he is.

'Having to rely on other people throughout your whole day means that everything has to be planned and there is no room for spontaneity. Nothing can explain the feeling inside me now when I wake up and know the day is mine; there beside me is the most willing carer you could ever dream of, tail always wagging. Instantly you go from the one who is cared for, to the one who is caring. Everything your dog needs comes from you; you exercise, feed, groom, play with and care for your dog. No matter how you feel in the morning or how much pain you are in, one look into those doggie eyes and it all disappears.

'I have always wanted to study art but felt before having Edward that I couldn't do this because I would be treated differently taking Peter as my carer. Since having Edward, I have completed two years at art college and passed my art and design level two.

'On one occasion Peter was in the garage and I decided to make him a cheese sandwich for dinner. I am never allowed to eat cheese as it is too dangerous, but for some reason I put a piece in my mouth to just suck it, but all of a sudden I swallowed and the cheese stuck fast in my throat. I could not breathe and hung onto the sink; all I could think was that I was going to die. I could feel my grip lessening on the sink and my legs giving way. The next thing I remember is that Peter was banging me on my back and telling me to cough, but I could not get enough air to cough. Eventually I was sick and the cheese came up again. I sat on the floor shaking and said how grateful I was that Peter had come in at that moment. It turned out that Peter had heard Edward barking, and opened the garage door to find Edward leaping in the air and running back and forth to the conservatory door. Edward had let himself

out of the kitchen and then out of the conservatory. Once in the garden he had run to the garage door. He barked and barked till Peter heard him. I am convinced that if Edward had not gone to get Peter, things would have had a terrible outcome; this act won Edward a PDSA Commendation, of which we are very proud. We now know without a shadow of doubt that we owe my life to one faithful, loyal dog: Edward.

'What was once a dream for me has become a reality thanks to Edward. I never thought I could be this happy. I have gone from being constantly afraid of what people think, to the outgoing and carefree person I am now thanks to Edward and Canine Partners. He has even been made the official mascot of the British Olympic Association medical team.

'I love Edward more than words can say; after all, I hold his lead and he holds my heart.'

## PAT DOGS (PETS AS THERAPY)

Pets as Therapy dogs are professional counsellors, but they do nothing more than what dogs are best at: providing attention. PAT dogs provide reassurance for those who need it most, or just someone who needs a smile. The biggest part of their eligibility (which is mostly down to natural behaviour) is just to be quiet and move without fast actions. PAT dogs are used all over world after natural disasters, in horrific situations such as the shooting in Connecticut in 2013, in

*Golden Retrievers have the ability to brighten our days, purely by showing unconditional love.*

churches, nursing homes, schools, hospitals and for victims of tragedy. Golden Retrievers make excellent PAT dogs; they are very calm and have a gentle disposition. They will happily sit with someone and be that shoulder to cry on, providing the unconditional love that makes them so easy to talk to.

Goldens have the unique ability to make every person feel special, whether they are family members or strangers; they will sit with someone, happily being stroked, until that person is ready to stop. They never judge or say anything back, seemingly having an understanding that they are needed.

Petting a dog can decrease stress, provide comfort and lower blood pressure. But PAT dogs give more than that; these special dogs seem to respond to emotion, even if nothing has been said. Dogs can read body language and have a sense of how someone is feeling, making it appear like they have empathy. If you have ever cried in front of a dog, you will know that they try to comfort you, either by licking you or just sitting quietly beside you. That reaction to our emotions only increases the amazing human–dog bond.

It is the simplicity that a dog can bring to those who need a friend, where there is no expectation from either dog or person; it is uncomplicated, unrivalled, unconditional love.

*The Golden Retriever is a loving, faithful companion.*

# CHAPTER 2

# A GOLDEN RETRIEVER FOR YOU

## READY FOR A DOG?

Many people love the idea of having a dog, and a Golden Retriever is often depicted as the 'family of four' addition that makes a lifestyle complete. A dog, however, is not a fashion accessory, nor a symbol of wealth or happiness; buying a dog is a huge commitment.

Before you decide to purchase a Golden Retriever, it is important to ask yourself why you want a Golden and whether you are suitable to have one? There are many factors to take into consideration, not least the inevitable costs, lifestyle changes, commitment and responsibility involved in owning a dog. The reward of owning a Golden Retriever is high, but if the timing is not suitable, it is better to have dog ownership as a future goal.

If you live alone, a Golden will provide endless affection and possibly much-needed companionship. Single people make excellent owners, as they quite often have more time to spend with their dog. However, in the case of a single owner with one dog, an intense relationship can result, which may lead to separation anxiety or jealous behaviour should you show affection to anyone else. Single owners often spoil their Goldens too, so watch out for over-feeding or allowing your Golden to rule the house.

Couples, too, make excellent Golden owners and give the dog a balanced relationship. There will, of course, be one person who naturally becomes the 'leader'. This is often the person who feeds, walks or spends the most time with the dog, so it is important that both owners spend time with the dog and that both join in with training and daily activities.

Couples with children, especially young children, tend to live very busy lives, which has its benefits

for dog ownership, but also its pitfalls. Goldens love to join in with family activities and make the perfect family pet, but if you do not make the time to raise your dog properly, you could end up with a boisterous and unruly adult Golden Retriever. If you want a puppy for your child to train, walk and grow up with, supervision must be carried out in the first year, as this period is crucial for instilling good household manners

*Golden Retrievers are beautiful in both looks and nature and are a popular choice for pets.*

*Encourage children to be gentle around dogs, and always supervise children with young puppies.*

(such as not begging for food at the table or jumping up), and leaving children to teach good behaviour may unintentionally allow bad habits to start. Children can overstimulate a young dog and coax him into games, which often get rough and end in tears when someone gets nipped.

## WHY CHOOSE A GOLDEN RETRIEVER

When people think of a dog, the Golden Retriever often comes to mind, and the breed is a popular choice as a family dog. They are sociable towards people and animals, intelligent and easy to train, excellent with children, gentle, kind and trustworthy by nature; they display a tolerant attitude, and are hard working with lots of stamina, eager to please, loyal, handsome, playful and generally well behaved.

There are, of course, two sides to every coin and the Golden Retriever also has some less appealing traits. Some can display a puppyish attitude well after they have turned one year old (which can be endearing but sometimes frustrating), and although they are exceptional with children, a young boisterous pup can easily knock over a small child. They can be quite lively and are easily bored, especially when young, which

*Even young Goldens show the wonderful characteristics of the breed. Here a young Golden waits calmly with her owner.*

*Goldens will draw attention to a new arrival at the house with a bark or howl, but they are not guard dogs.*

*Golden Retrievers love to go everywhere with you.*

may turn into destructive tendencies, and they can display a stubborn streak on occasion. Goldens are not guard dogs: after the initial bark, they are more likely to welcome any intruder with their favourite toys. They shed profusely and their hair will get everywhere, even in places your Golden has never been, so they are not a good choice for the house proud! Likewise, Goldens have a real love for water, so if you want a dog who will stay clean on a walk, then a Golden is not for you; they are bound to find the one puddle in the entire vicinity. Lastly, Goldens love to eat and can easily gain weight if their diet is not monitored.

Every dog is an individual personality, but there are aspects that are special to each breed. Goldens have no shortage of traits that make them especially endearing and these often outweigh any negative points; these include a friendly greeting, a charming outlook, a loyal and understanding companion, a desire to bring you presents (whether wanted or not) and their need to be involved with the family. To a Golden Retriever it doesn't matter if you're not going anywhere interesting; they're always joyful, with an uplifting attitude, a wagging tail and a happy heart.

## CHOOSING YOUR GOLDEN RETRIEVER

Choosing the right dog for you is exciting but it can also be a difficult decision. First, you need to decide whether you would like a puppy or an older dog.

If you have decided you want a puppy, you must ensure you are doing so for the right reasons; all puppies are small, cute and vulnerable, and it is easy to fall in love with any puppy without really considering the implications of owning one. Costs aside, puppies require a lot of your attention to keep them out of mischief and you will have to take into account that there will be accidents, whether that is toileting in the house or chewing the furniture.

Older dogs are often overlooked compared to puppies, but they make wonderful pets; often they have been trained beforehand and you do not have to go through toilet training, chewing, play biting, socializing, obedience training and learning house rules, which are often the most testing times for a puppy owner. It

*Golden puppies are appealing, with a Polar Bear appearance!*

*Adult dogs make excellent pets and come without the puppy issues. Getting an adult dog does not mean they will not have a playful streak.*

does not mean, however, that an older dog will come without any of the problems associated with puppies; you may still arrive home to find your soft furnishings ripped apart. Training your new companion is required, whether young or old.

Whether you want a puppy or an older dog, you will be taking on a new family member who will be completely dependent on you. It is not a decision to take lightly and you must be committed to looking after and caring for your dog throughout his life. Every person who will be involved in the dog's life should be consulted before getting your new dog to ensure everyone is happy with the decision.

Children should also be involved when choosing a dog, as children and dogs often build strong bonds. Children frequently want a dog more than anyone else in the family and it is a great way for them to learn how to care for an animal. My own fondest childhood

*Everyone should be involved when choosing a puppy, so everyone is happy with the decision.*

very long flat coat, while others are wavier. Traditionally, the golden coat was more popular among working dogs, and the cream for show dogs, but the colour of coat will not predict the behaviour of your dog or mean he is more suitable for one lifestyle than another.

memories involve the family dog (and my family too, of course). As Robert Benchley said, 'Every boy should have two things: a dog and a mother who lets him have one.'

*A male Golden with the traditional rich golden coat.*

## CREAM OR GOLDEN?

The coat of a Golden Retriever comes in a variety of golden and cream shades. The choice of colour is down to personal preference. Some owners like the cream colouring as they have a forever young look about them, whereas others like the traditional golden coat. The choice is yours, but bear in mind, if you are buying a puppy, that the coat may change colour as he develops. The best guide to the final coat colour is to look at the parents' coats, as most puppies take after them in looks. The texture of the coat varies also; some have a

## SEXES

Selecting a dog or bitch is a matter of personal preference; both have characteristic traits that will appeal to some owners and put others off. Male dogs often grow bigger than females and are usually more outgoing; as they develop and reach puberty, masculine behaviour will peak, which can affect training and cause problems. Females are smaller and more sensitive, but something to bear in mind is that bitches will have a season every six months or so, which can be quite messy, especially if you have carpets, and it may potentially affect behaviour. Depending on the individual dog, some bitches can also have phantom pregnancies which often lead to nesting, becoming possessive over items and lactating, which will require veterinary attention.

## NEUTERING

Neutering means castration (removal of the testes) in a dog or spaying (removal of the ovaries and uterus) in a bitch. If you do not intend to breed from your dog,

having him castrated will reduce any unwanted tendencies such as roaming, potential dominance behaviour towards other dogs, territory marking and hypersexual behaviour.

Puberty for a dog occurs at around nine months old. Some dogs may not show any of the behavioural problems listed above and so castration may not be necessary, apart from providing peace of mind. Castration involves the removal of both testes under general anaesthetic. There will be a few dissolvable stitches which will need checking approximately seven days

*The difference between golden-coated and cream-coated Golden Retrievers. Here both dogs have a wave to the coat.*

later, and some fur will have been shaved where the anaesthetic injections were given and where the incision was made.

Likewise, if you do not intend to breed from your bitch, having her spayed will stop any seasons, unplanned pregnancies, phantom pregnancies and womb infections, and reduces the risk of mammary tumours later in life. One downside to spaying a Golden is that the soft texture of the coat is lost, and is replaced with a curlier, coarser coat. It is advised that bitches are spayed after their first season and three months after a season, because the womb has a lower blood supply at that time, making it less traumatic. Spaying involves the surgical removal of both ovaries and the uterus through an incision in the midline of the abdomen under general anaesthetic. As with castration, there will be a few dissolvable stitches that will need checking seven days later and some fur shaved where the anaesthetic injections were given and the incision made.

After the operation, your dog will be drowsy for a few hours until the sedation wears off. A small bland meal can be offered in the evening but do not worry if the dog refuses food altogether. Some dogs whimper, howl or cry after the operation, but it is important not to be tempted to give them more painkillers than prescribed by your vet. Ensure your dog has somewhere comfortable and quiet to rest; she should take it easy for about ten days after the operation, during which time only short walks on a lead are advisable If your dog starts to lick, scratch or chew at the stitching, a cone collar can be fitted to stop her from reaching it.

After neutering, there is a tendency for dogs to gain weight; this is mainly due to the reduction in sex hormones and the metabolic rate. This should be carefully monitored, and a reduced diet considered if necessary.

## GOLDEN RETRIEVER CROSSES

Many different breeds of dog make excellent pets, but if you want a Golden Retriever cross, do bear in mind that, as with any crossbreed, there is no guarantee what you will end up with if buying a puppy. Buying a crossbreed does not mean you are getting a healthier dog either, as if the health problem is genetic, the potential of it being passed from the parents to the puppy will still exist, no matter what the breed of dog. The most common cross with a Golden Retriever is with a Standard Poodle, aptly named a 'Golden Doodle'. The original intention of this cross was to produce a pet with the intelligence of both breeds, the sound temperament of a Golden and the non-moulting coat of the Poodle. However, having a Golden Doodle does not necessarily mean you will get the best of both breeds; I have on several occasions seen these crosses becoming larger than both breeds; they are very excitable and moult heavily. Both Goldens and Poodles are also prone to Hip Dysplasia, so ensure that any breeder has had both parents hip scored before purchasing a puppy.

Good breeders of these crosses will choose first generation breeding (F1) and first generation cross back (F1B) only, which will increase genetic diversity. F1 breeding of a Golden Doodle means the breeding of a purebred Golden Retriever with a purebred Standard Poodle. F1B is the breeding between a Golden Doodle and a purebred Golden Retriever. (F2 breeding is the breeding of two Golden Doodles.)

When choosing a Golden crossbreed, be very careful about what the dog is crossed with, and if picking a puppy, ask to see both parents. Some unscrupulous breeders will charge a large sum of money for 'designer dogs' in order to take advantage of these dogs' current popularity, but without any consideration for the health and welfare of the dogs and puppies.

## CHAPTER 3

# FINDING YOUR GOLDEN RETRIEVER

## BREEDERS

It is always best to purchase a puppy directly from a reputable breeder. The Kennel Club's website provides a list of Assured Breeders in your area. Buying a puppy from an Assured Breeder means the puppy will be registered with the Kennel Club and that the breeder is following Kennel Club policies on breeding by carrying out relevant health screening, providing written advice on socialization, feeding, worming, exercise and vaccinations, providing reasonable post-sale advice and drawing up a contract of sale. A good breeder will have planned the litter, and chosen the stud dog and bitch carefully before mating, ensuring both are of sound temperament and exemplary pedigree (calculating the inbreeding coefficients), and have had all the relevant health tests.

Not all breeders raise their puppies in the same way, so it is vital that you ask lots of questions about how the puppies have been raised, and that you see the litter and their mother in their environment. The best possible start for a puppy is to be born in a house full of activity, where he can experience household noises, sights and smells, be handled regularly and meet lots of new people. This socialization from an early age will prove advantageous when settling your new puppy into your home, starting training and expanding his socialization.

*Ask lots of questions about the puppies and the breeder before committing to buy one.*

## PET SHOPS/PUPPY FARMS/DEALERS

Puppy farm dogs are bred en masse, and are often born in unsuitable environments without any care or consideration for the mother or the litter. These puppies are produced without any thought for their welfare and frequently pass through many hands before they arrive at their new home. Puppy farm dogs are also more likely to have temperamental and health problems later in life.

It is very tempting to want to 'rescue' these puppies from their bad start in life, but doing so simply encourages these dealers to produce more puppies to meet the demand. To make sure you are not buying a puppy farm dog, always go and visit the breeder at the place where the puppy has been brought up. Never buy a puppy if:

- you cannot see where the puppy has been reared;
- you cannot see the mother of the litter;
- the breeder offers to meet you somewhere, or says they will deliver the puppy to you;
- the breeder has a variety of different puppies available; or
- you have *any* doubts over the breeder or the puppy.

## RESCUE CENTRES/FOSTER HOMES

Rescuing a dog is both hugely gratifying and admirable. There are a number of different rescue organizations, including breed-specific ones, around the country. Looking for a rescue Golden Retriever in the mainstream organizations may prove quite difficult as they are very popular and are often rehomed quite quickly. To ensure you find the best Golden Retriever for you, contact a breed-specific rescue organization, which means you can narrow your search to just rescue organizations for Golden Retrievers. Not only are the people who run them experts in the breed, but they will be able to match you with a suitable dog. One of the benefits of these breed-specific rescues is that the dogs are often cared for in foster homes rather than brought into kennels. Fostering helps reduce stress and provides a happy environment for the dog before he finds a new permanent home. Occasionally

*Giving an older Golden a second chance can be a very fulfilling experience.*

puppies can also be sourced through breed-specific rescue organizations, but the majority are older dogs. The Kennel Club's website provides a list of all breed-specific rescue organizations, along with their contact details and links to websites.

## SELECTING YOUR GOLDEN: FROM BREEDERS

Selecting a puppy from a litter is difficult, especially if you are lucky enough to have first choice. This is where knowing whether you want a male or female helps, as it narrows the choice. You will be able to select your puppy when he is six to eight weeks old. A puppy that is confident, happy to be handled and approaches you is likely to become a well-rounded dog, and is a better choice than a puppy that is shy and cowers when you try to touch him. A puppy that is concerned about people, is hand shy or fearful will require more training and socialization to overcome his fears, and such behaviour in a puppy can be an indicator of fearful behaviour in the future. In contrast, a puppy that is confident can be more easily trained and will settle into his new home and pick up life skills more quickly.

A healthy puppy should be active with bright eyes and no signs of discharge; he should respond to noises, have a moist (but not runny) nose, clean, sweet-smelling ears and a shiny coat with no bald patches or sores.

A puppy's behaviour is not moulded just through the way he is reared, but is part of his genetics; if the mother has a nice temperament, it is a good indication that your puppy will have a nice well balanced temperament as he gets older. Be wary if the breeder says that you cannot see the mother because she has become aggressive towards strangers since having the puppies; although stress can trigger behavioural issues, only females with completely sound temperaments should be bred from, so it is better, especially if you may want to breed in the future, to avoid her puppies.

Take your time over choosing your puppy and make sure you have selected the right one for you and your family; a good breeder will allow you plenty of time to do this. Once you have chosen your puppy, ideally try to see him again before bringing him home. You need to be sure you have chosen the right one, and he needs to get to know you a little better before you take him

*Take your time when choosing a puppy and meet him several times if possible before taking him home.*

home, as going home with total strangers will be quite frightening to a small puppy.

### Showing and Working

If you have decided that you wish to show your dog in the future, it is especially important to select the right puppy. First, there is a distinct difference between show-type and working-type Goldens. The most obvious difference is the colouring, with show dogs having a lighter, more cream-coloured and fuller coat, and being larger and more squarely built than the working type. Both types enjoy an active lifestyle, and should have the same biddable and laid-back temperament, although working types can be more driven and require more mental stimulation and training. Whether you are looking for a show or working type, responsible breeders should have had their breeding stock screened for both hip dysplasia and eye problems, and ideally also for elbow dysplasia, Progressive Retinal Atrophy (PRA) and DNA-tested for Ichthyosis.

For a potential show dog, choose a breeder using showing bloodlines; a bloodline is normally defined by a kennel name, which is registered with the Kennel Club and is linked as a type of branding to a particular 'kennel' or breeder. Multiple people can share a kennel name and dogs with different breeding can all 'belong' to a kennel name; it does not necessarily mean the dogs are related because they share the same kennel name. If the breeder has a kennel name, you can research it to see their achievements in showing. Look to see whether there are lots of champions in the bloodline; this can be easily done by looking at a five-generation pedigree, where the letters CH will occur next to the name of the dog. Remember that whether the bloodline has many champions or few, health and temperament are the most important factors to take into consideration when choosing a puppy.

For both showing and field trials, the puppy must be registered with the Kennel Club and transferred into your ownership.

Whether for working or show, male pups should have two normal testicles (your vet will be able to tell you if you're not sure). For showing, dogs should be left entire, unless it is likely to be detrimental to their

*Your breeder will be able to advise which puppy shows signs of being suitable for showing.*

health, whereas dogs participating in field trials will not be penalized for being neutered.

The working-type Golden is typically a darker gold in colour with a shorter coat and more slender appearance, which makes retrieving game on land and in the water easy. If you are looking for a working dog, then select working bloodlines and look out for any field trial winners and champions (FTCH next to the name of the dogs) on the pedigree. Not many kennels breed both showing and working dogs, and the show type is becoming the more popular of the two.

The breeder should be able to give you the best advice for selecting a show or working puppy. Breeders with lots of experience will rank the puppies with the most potential for the show ring or in field trials. Some may even pick a puppy for you if you explain exactly what you are looking for, as no one will know the puppies as well as the breeder does in terms of temperament. It is always very difficult to say which puppy will have the most potential in adulthood, but there are some tell-tale signs; for showing, for example, the puppy should show promise to fit the breed standard. For gundog work, the puppy should be alert, naturally inquisitive and confident. Above everything must come good temperament, for that is what makes the Golden Retriever the iconic

dog it has become, whether as a show dog, working dog or family pet.

## SELECTING YOUR GOLDEN: RESCUE CENTRES

Selecting your Golden Retriever from a rescue organization can be difficult as there are many beautiful dogs that will give you those sad eyes, and you will want to take them all home. As hard as it may be, don't just pick the one with the worst background, or the one who has been in rescue for the longest time. The most important thing to consider when selecting your rescue dog is finding the most suitable one for you. You will be asked lots of questions by the staff about you and your lifestyle, and perhaps asked to fill out a questionnaire to ensure a suitable dog is found for you. Talk to the staff who work at the rescue organization and know the dogs best, as some dogs will have behavioural issues. If you have children or perhaps another dog, selecting a dog that is well behaved and familiar with both would be a safer choice than selecting one who has had little or no contact with families.

Once you have selected a dog, ensure you are allowed plenty of time to get to know the dog and vice versa. Depending on the organization you select your dog from, the very least you will be able to do is take the dog out for a walk. Bring the whole family to meet and walk the dog so everyone is happy with the choice. Ask if you can meet and walk the dog several times before making a choice. Once the decision is made, the organization should carry out a home check, which often involves a home visit and more questions. As soon as the home check is approved, you will be allowed to bring your new family member home. Many rescue organizations allow for a trial period, and may contact you several weeks or months down the line to confirm that the dog has settled into the home and everyone is happy.

*The time it takes for a Golden to settle into his new home will depend on the individual dog; spend plenty of time with him to help him.*

# CHAPTER 4

# THE NEW ADDITION

## COST

Golden Retrievers are not the most expensive breed of pedigree dog to purchase, but it is important to remember that if you buy a dog on the cheap, you will get what you pay for. A pedigree, registered puppy will cost approximately £300–£500, while for a puppy from top showing or working bloodlines you can expect to pay up to twice that amount. As they gain in popularity, Golden crosses can often cost as much as pedigree dogs. Expect to pay around £150–£300 for puppies from 'accidental' litters. Rescue centres charge a rehoming fee for puppies and dogs, which can vary from £50–£150 depending on the rescue centre.

As well as the initial outlay of buying a new dog, there are yearly and monthly costs to take into consideration, including insurance, food, toys, equipment and bedding, and regular veterinary treatments such as worming, plus grooming, pet sitting and kennels (when required).

## LIFESTYLE

Before bringing home your new family member, it is important to take into consideration how he will fit into your lifestyle. If you work, or are out for more than four hours of the day, it is best to plan ahead to see what options are available for when you're at work, away or perhaps even on holiday, and what the implications are.

Doggy day care is where your dog goes to someone's house or established set-up for the day, normally with other dogs. It is the equivalent of a day crèche and, depending on what is available near you, may offer various services and facilities. In the most basic set-up your dog will spend the day in someone's home, garden or kennel, while at the other end of the scale there may be an established arena with toys, games, pens and a number of staff. Some daycare centres also offer a pick-up and drop-off service, grooming, walking and more, at an additional cost. If this is an option you are interested in, find out what is included and see where your dog will be kept during the day. If your dog will be kept with others, he must behave well around other dogs but make sure there will be someone to supervise them at all times. Playing with other dogs is great for socialization and has the benefit that your dog gets lots of exercise! Some daycare centres may insist that your dog has some level of basic training so he does not become a nuisance if

### Top Tip

A dog will cost on average £150 a month to keep, so work out whether you can afford to have a dog and still cover any unforeseen costs. This average cost is for guidance only and covers food, insurance, equipment, veterinary prescriptions (worming, flea treatments) on a monthly basis, but the figure can vary greatly depending on individual circumstances. Many dogs are rehomed every year because the monthly outgoings become too high. There are also other factors to take into consideration, such as pet sitters, kennels and extra veterinary fees that can substantially increase the monthly cost.

*Goldens can adapt into any lifestyle.*

unruly. Depending on the area, services and facilities available, you could be looking at a cost of £5–£25 a day.

The most popular and convenient daily option is a pet sitter, where an individual comes to your house and lets your dogs out, normally just in your garden to relieve themselves, although some may offer a walk. Pet sitters normally stay for anywhere between ten minutes and an hour, and you can expect to pay £5–£12 per visit. Some pet sitters may also offer multiple services, such as cleaning, ironing or even gardening.

Dog walkers normally come to your house, collect your dog and take him to a nearby park or equivalent for a walk, usually with other dogs. It is important that the dog walker builds up a relationship with your dog before taking him on a walk. If the dog walker intends to let the dogs off the lead, you need to know that your dog will respond to their commands. Before choosing a dog walker, it is important to know where your dog is being walked and with how many dogs. A good dog walker will not take too many dogs at one time so they can always be in control if anything happens. Do also check their insurance to see whether they will take responsibility should anything happen to your dog during the time in which they are being walked. The cost of dog walking is £5–£12 per walk (normally an hour). Although the cost difference is sometimes minimal between a dog walker and a pet sitter, there are more risk implications for someone else walking your dog.

Going away on holiday is increasingly expensive and, if you are not taking your dog with you, costs can increase even further. The cheapest (or even free) option is to find a neighbour, friend or relative who will look after your dog for you. Alternatively, you may know a student who wants to earn a little extra cash over holiday breaks.

Kennels are the most obvious option for most owners; it is also normally one of the cheapest, unless there is a kennel of excellent standards and multiple services. Always go and visit a kennel before booking your dog in, as you need to know that your dog will be looked after properly, exercised adequately and his requirements met, and that the facilities are suitable. Your dog's booster vaccinations must be up-to-date, he should also have had a kennel cough vaccination. It is also worth worming and applying flea treatment both before and after your dog is kennelled. The average cost at kennels for a medium–large dog is £15–20 a day as standard.

If, like many people, you are not taken with the idea of leaving your dog in kennels, a house sitter is an increasingly popular option. House sitting is where someone stays in your house for the period you are away. There are multiple benefits to this: your dog is looked after in the comfort of his own home and his routine is not disturbed, plants will be watered, and there is the additional security of someone being in your home, generally keeping an eye on things. Make sure you meet the person who will be staying in your home while you are away and ensure they have emergency contact details should anything happen. This option may be more cost-effective and convenient if you have several pets, but expect to pay £25–£40 a day on average.

Another option is similar to a day crèche but for overnight stays, normally in someone's home. Again, see where your dog will be staying, check where he will be sleeping, and find out whether he will be left alone at any point or if other dogs will be there. Expect to pay £10–£20 a day.

## PREPARATION

Whether you are bringing home a puppy or an older

*On the day you pick up your puppy, ask if you can have a piece of bedding that smells like his littermates (if you haven't supplied your own beforehand).*

dog, various items and equipment should be purchased before his arrival. These items include, but are not limited to:

- a suitable dog bed
- a puppy pen or crate
- water and feeding bowls
- collar and lead; most puppy collars are adjustable but if you are acquiring an older dog, wait until he is home before purchasing a new collar to ensure you buy the correct size
- toys
- treats
- dog food

- grooming equipment
- towels
- shampoo suitable for dogs
- old newspapers for toileting
- a first aid kit suitable for dogs

Other things you should do before you bring your puppy or dog home include registering with your local vet and obtaining suitable pet insurance (if needed).

If you live in a terraced or semi-detached house, or have neighbours living close by, it is neighbourly to let them know that you are bringing home a new addition to the family and ask that they keep you informed should there be too much noise. Remember that not everyone likes dogs and may not be as receptive to the idea as you are.

On the day of collection of your puppy or dog, leave in plenty of time so there is no rush. It will be very exciting for everyone, so making sure you are prepared by reducing any housework or chores to come home to will ensure that your new addition will have your undivided attention on the first day.

## RESPONSIBILITY

There are a number of laws about which, as a dog owner, you should be aware. The laws most likely to affect you are described below.

### Animal Welfare Act 2006

This Act was introduced in 2007 and covers the measures put in place to stop animal cruelty, neglect, mutilation, tail docking, animal fighting and the giving away of pets as prizes. It also specifies a duty of care, which lays down that each owner must provide for their animal a suitable environment, a suitable diet, the ability to exhibit normal behaviour, protection from pain,

*Bringing your puppy home is one of the most exciting times, so make sure you are well prepared for your new arrival.*

undue suffering, injury and disease, and consideration of the animal's needs.

### The Clean Neighbourhoods and Environment Act 2005

This Act has brought into legislation the ability to fine an owner up to £1,000 for breaching dog control orders. Your local authority can specify the offences, which include: failing to remove dog faeces, not keeping a dog on a lead, not putting a dog on a lead when directed to do so, permitting a dog to enter land where dogs are excluded, and taking more than a specified number of dogs on to land. Also included in this Act is the legislation on stray dogs, by which any stray dogs picked up by the police shall be transferred to and the responsibility of the local authority. Dog wardens are obliged to take hold of any stray dog, and it is illegal to take a stray dog into your home without reporting it to the police.

If a dog persistently barks and causes a nuisance to neighbours, the local authority can issue a noise abatement notice. If the notice is not followed, the owner may be liable to pay fees and legal expenses.

### Breeding and Sales of Dogs (Welfare) Act 1998

Breeders who produce more than five litters a year must obtain a licence through their local authority. Licensed breeders must follow these guidelines:

- Do not mate a bitch under the age of twelve months
- Do not breed more than six litters from one bitch
- Do not breed two litters from the same bitch within a twelve-month period
- Keep up to date and accurate records
- Do not sell a puppy until it is at least eight weeks old.

### The Control of Dogs Order 1992

This Act covers the requirement that any dog in a public place must wear a collar with the name and address of the owner engraved or written on a dog tag. This law is currently under government revision, looking at adding mandatory microchipping for all dogs by 2016.

### Dangerous Dogs Act 1991 (including 2014 amendment)

This Act states that it is a criminal offence to allow a dog to be dangerously out of control in a public place, to be in a place the dog is not permitted to be and (as of 2014) on private property. A dangerous dog is defined as a dog that has caused injury to someone.

A complaint may be issued by someone even if your dog only barks at, chases or jumps up at them. A dog doesn't have to bite to be deemed dangerous, so it is vital that your dog is trained correctly and under control at all times.

If your dog causes injury to someone, he may be seized immediately by the police and automatically destroyed (unless a court says otherwise). As the owner, you may face a ban on keeping dogs, be given a prison sentence and/or have to pay a fine and compensation.

### Pet Travel Scheme 2000

This scheme came into being to prevent rabies, other diseases and tapeworm from entering the UK when dogs are imported. Before pets are allowed into the UK, they have to meet certain health criteria. A dog may enter or return to the UK twenty-one days after vaccination, and treatment for tapeworm must be carried out twenty-four hours to five days before travelling. If a dog is coming from outside the EU a blood test must be carried out post-vaccination and the dog quarantined for three months before entering the UK.

### The Road Traffic Act 1988

Under this Act it is an offence to allow a dog on a road without it being on a lead. If your dog is injured in a car accident, the driver of the vehicle must stop and give their details to the owner or person responsible for the dog.

### Dogs (Protection of Livestock) Act 1953

This Act states that your dog must not cause distress, chase or attack any livestock on agricultural land. Dogs must be kept on a lead around livestock (if you do not own the livestock). If farmers deem your dog to be causing distress to livestock, they have the right to stop him (even by means of shooting the dog in certain circumstances).

## BRINGING YOUR PUPPY HOME

Puppies can go home at eight weeks of age or older. There are many opinions on when a puppy can leave, and there are advantages and disadvantages to taking a puppy too soon or too late. The best time on average is around eight weeks of age. The day you bring your new family member home is very exciting. Ensure your car is packed with all the things you need for your dog:

- water
- blankets/bed
- waste bags
- collar/lead
- toys

Puppies may not have experienced car journeys, and older dogs may not enjoy travelling. With this in mind, ensure the journey is as smooth as possible; keep music at a low level and make sure there is ventilation in the car. You may prefer to place a puppy on a passenger's lap for the journey, where he can be kept calm and secure.

As tempting as it is to show off your new arrival, the puppy will be overwhelmed if your house is full of new people when he comes home. Try not to have too many visitors in the first few days to allow your puppy to settle and get to know you. Keep the environment calm and relatively quiet.

When you arrive at your house, bring your puppy/dog inside and allow him to have a good sniff around to get used to his new surroundings. Do not leave him unattended, and watch to see his reaction to things. Puppies will probably be a little nervous at first. Do not pick him up; just let him take in the environment. Even if your puppy or older dog has been living in a house beforehand, it does not necessarily mean he will know your house rules, so after he has inspected the house let him go outside to relieve himself and explore your garden.

Introduce your puppy to his new toys and allow him to play with them. Show your puppy his sleeping area, so he knows where to go if he wants to rest; make sure it is warm and comfortable as he will miss the warmth and security of his mother and siblings; try putting a cuddly toy in the bed as a companion.

*Allow your puppy time to explore his new environment.*

**Top Tip**

From the day you bring your puppy/dog home, arrange your daily routine to include the new addition. Adopt feeding times and play/walk times that are suitable for you. Golden Retrievers, whether young or old, will appreciate a routine, especially when they are new to the household, as it will help them settle more quickly. Remember that young puppies should not be allowed to go outside (apart from in your garden) or to meet any non-family dogs until they have had both vaccinations.

*Puppies will explore every possible corner of your house and garden.*

*Introduce your puppy to existing dogs in the household in a neutral space.*

Your puppy may be too overwhelmed to eat on the first night, so don't worry too much. Do not try to force him to eat. If he scoffs down his food, allow him space to eat and don't try to slow him down (puppies are used to competing for food with their siblings, so this is perfectly normal).

## REGISTERING

If you have purchased a Kennel Club registered puppy, it is important that you change the ownership of the puppy. This is especially true if you intend to show or breed from your dog as you will not be able to enter shows or register any offspring if your dog is not listed in the correct ownership. Your dog will remain registered in the breeder's name until you register him.

Registering your puppy in your name can be done using the transfer form supplied by the breeder or online using the unique code printed on the transfer form. You can also purchase a three- or five-generation pedigree at the same time, if not supplied by the breeder, which will show your dog's family tree.

When you pick up your puppy from the breeder, ensure you collect the paperwork at the same time and ask whether there are any endorsements placed on the puppy. These have the power to prevent you showing or registering your dog abroad, or registering any offspring your puppy may have in the future.

Endorsements can only be lifted by the person(s) who placed them (normally the breeder). The breeder may have criteria that must be met before they will consider lifting any endorsements; this should be discussed and covered in the contract before taking the puppy home.

## ANOTHER DOG IN THE HOUSE

If you have another dog in the household, bringing a new puppy or dog in can be a great benefit to both dogs, but it can also cause problems.

Watch very carefully as you introduce your new dog. Arrange for them to meet outside the house, either in the garden or in a field/park nearby, and then walk them back together. Do not leave them alone together, make sure all toys are put away when they are not being played with and engage in bonding activities such as playing and going for walks to encourage a bond between them. Always remember that introductions must be done carefully and at a pace suitable for both dogs.

A second dog will provide companionship for the first, and they will instantly have a friend who speaks the same language. Older dogs also make great teachers, as long as they are well behaved themselves. The disadvantage is that a puppy may relate more to the older dog and thus will be less willing to listen to you. Two or more dogs build a very strong bond, so when you are training it is important that the dogs are separated so there are no distractions for the new dog. It is also important to spend some time playing with your new dog alone; this allows time for the new puppy/dog to bond with you too. Of course, both dogs can play with each other and other dogs too, as it is important for socialization, but this playtime must be limited as the new puppy needs to learn the way of the family and your rules and boundaries.

Once the dogs have established a good bond, do not interfere if your older dog disciplines the new arrival by growling or snapping at him. Only intervene if you fear for your puppy's safety. Sometimes your older dog needs to have his own rules, and he should be allowed to do that. If you interfere, you will alter the relationship they have.

## OTHER PETS

It can be very beneficial if you have other pets in the household, such as cats or small animals, as dogs love to chase both; being well socialized will teach your puppy self-control and appropriate behaviour towards other species. A puppy will accept an introduction to a new pet more easily than an older dog, unless he previously lived with small animals or cats.

If you have a cat, put the puppy/dog on a lead so the cat can get to know the dog without being ambushed or feeling threatened by the new arrival. If a dog has had little or no previous contact with different species, the instinct to chase, catch and kill can sometimes be overwhelming, so it is important to have your dog under control.

*Introduce your puppy gradually to all your pets to ensure harmonious living.*

The introduction of a new puppy/dog must be minimal and gradual, and your dog should never be left alone with a cat if they have not built up a good relationship. No dog (or cat, for that matter) should be trusted with a small animal of any sort; with any small, fast-moving animal, the natural instinct to chase often takes over – and if they do it once, they soon realize how much fun it is, and it can be a hard habit to break.

## MORE THAN ONE PUPPY

Before taking on more than one puppy at the same time, ask yourself why you want to get two pups. The most popular answers to this question are that they can keep each other company and will be best friends for life, and that a couple or children can have one puppy each. These answers may be true, but there are arguments against them.

Yes, they will keep each other company, especially when you are out, but separation anxiety can still happen and dogs should not be left for long periods of time just because they have a companion to lighten the load. There is also the danger that this constant companionship means that they become inseparable.

The notion of two people or children having one puppy each is fine in theory, but only rarely will a puppy develop the desired human–dog bond with the 'correct' owner, unless the puppy is allowed more one-on-one time with that person than with the other puppy. Often what actually happens is that the puppies build such a strong bond with each other that they do not bond with their owner, or will only listen to one person, normally the person who spends the most time with them (mum or dad if the puppies are being bought for children). If you are considering buying each child a puppy, bear in mind the implications of who will be looking

*Two dogs will often form close bonds with one another.*

**Top Tip**

New puppies, whether you decide to have one or two, present certain challenges and will require your time and energy. Puppies are hard work as it is, but there are also costs to take into consideration. The first year is often the most expensive, with all the implications that come with having a puppy, but you should also look at what having two older dogs will cost, especially if they both require medical attention in later life.

Having two dogs will at least double your monthly costs, and there are other considerations to take into account before getting more than one dog, which may not necessarily be cost-related:

- larger food bills;
- larger veterinary fees;
- whether kennels/pet sitters will look after more than one dog and what it will cost;
- whether your car is big enough for two dogs. (Goldens are large dogs and there will come a point where you need to take both dogs – or more! – in the car at the same time. Can you afford a larger vehicle?);
- whether you can comfortably walk both dogs at the same time. Can others, if required?;
- are there any restrictions to having more than one dog?; and
- is your house/garden large enough to accommodate more than one Golden?

*Goldens can become addictive and many owners will go on to have more than one dog.*

after the puppies for the majority of the time. While older children may fulfil their promises to walk, feed, look after and train their puppy, younger children may not be able to handle such a large dog. Even though Goldens are extremely good with children, boisterous large puppies will knock a young child over, may jump up and ignore non-authoritative commands, and soon two sweet puppies can become two unruly teenagers.

The idea that two puppies brought up together from puppyhood will be best friends for life is not necessarily true. They may be best friends as puppies, but that does not mean they will be best friends as adults. Siblings play and fight like siblings; they are often rough with one another and can be competitive or protective of valuables such as toys and food. At the other end of the scale, such dogs can become over-reliant on one another, and lose confidence as individuals without their best friend.

Puppies need time to bond with their new owners, so if you get two you should walk them, train them and play with them individually. This will build their confidence as individual dogs without the need for their litter mate. You do not need to do this for their whole lives, just for the first year so they can not only bond with, but will listen to their owner. Teach commands individually to begin with, before bringing the puppies together, and then teach the puppies to carry out the commands at the same time. They may not learn at the same rate, though, so it is important to treat each as an individual and only bring them together for training when they are both on the same page. There is no point asking both dogs to jump through hoops if one has only just learnt how to sit.

Rearing two puppies individually in this way will take twice as long and be twice as hard as rearing just one, but the outcome will be two well-behaved dogs; trying to do everything with them together will make it very hard to get and retain their attention, and thus they will be difficult to train.

Done correctly, it will go from double the mess, double the hard work and double the exhaustion to double the love, double the cuddles and double the friendship.

# CHAPTER 5

# PUPPY LOVE

## THE FIRST NIGHT

Crate training is becoming more popular with owners, not least because it provides peace of mind from knowing that your puppy is not doing any harm to himself, nor causing mischief when left unattended. Used correctly, crates can provide your puppy with his own warm, secure and safe den that he will be happy to relax in.

The crate should be large enough so your puppy can stand up, stretch out and move around comfortably.

Remember that puppies don't stay small for long, so ensure the crate will be large enough as your puppy grows. When selecting your crate, be mindful of the space between the bars; your puppy should not be able to get his legs or his jaws caught easily.

Make sure the crate is placed somewhere where your puppy can still feel part of the family; the kitchen or family room are the most suitable areas. A regular wipe-down of the crate floor and airing of the bedding will ensure the crate is always clean, comfortable and warm.

*Puppies will fall asleep almost anywhere.*

To introduce your puppy to the crate, begin by leaving the door open and encouraging him to investigate. Never push your puppy into the crate as it will instantly become a negative experience. If your puppy goes inside, do not close the door behind him as this may cause anxiety if he feels confined, and may potentially cause injury if he tries to jump up or bite the bars. Instead, spend time associating the crate with good things, such as placing food and toys inside for your puppy. When he is showing signs of relaxing inside the crate, only then should the door be pushed closed and reopened while he remains calm. It may take practice and some patience, but a puppy that is happy to go into his crate is more likely to settle quickly when it comes to bedtime.

Once your puppy is happy to go and settle in his crate, you can begin leaving him to sleep in there. If he is going to be left unattended, place the bed on one side of the crate and put paper down on the other, so your puppy can relieve himself without soiling his bed. Having only a bed in the crate may prevent your puppy from toileting on his bed, but a desperate puppy will go regardless, so it is best to provide a separate area. Ideally, if your puppy needs to go out and you are with him, you should let him out of the crate and take him straight outside to relieve himself.

Before bedtime, provide a little playtime if your puppy is showing no signs of tiring, then take him outside to go to the toilet. Once back inside, wind down by dimming lights or turning them off, and keeping volumes low; this will instigate a pattern of when bedtime is. When your puppy starts to show signs of relaxing, take him to the area he will be sleeping in.

Bringing the crate into your bedroom at night can provide comfort. It is not a matter of right or wrong in having your dog sleep with you or away from you, but rather a matter of personal preference. An older dog may wish to sleep on his own but puppies are very dependent and will cry for you, sometimes for many hours. Bear in mind that puppies are not used to sleeping on their own and it is only natural for them to want to be amongst the rest of the pack for safety and security. Having your puppy sleep in your bedroom with you while he gets used to your routine can also encourage him to follow your sleeping patterns. Do not allow very young puppies to sleep on your bed; they can easily roll off the edge and hurt themselves from a high fall. If you want your puppy to sleep on your bed when he is older, place his bed beside yours until he is old enough to jump on and off the bed with ease.

If your puppy will be sleeping in a separate room from you, make the room dark and comfortably warm, or place a blanket over the top of the crate. Try leaving soft music on in the background or placing a clock near the crate, which can help to soothe him to sleep.

Your puppy will probably cry for a while when you leave him, but, as tempting as it is, it is best not to make a fuss. Don't keep going downstairs to check on him or your puppy will soon learn that when he cries, you come to him, and this will only encourage him. Only once he has calmed down a little should you go and let him out, without creating too much of a big deal out of it. If your puppy cries in the middle of the night, see if he needs the toilet by taking him outside, but without encouraging too much excitement. As soon as your puppy has been to the toilet, put him back to bed. If he has fully woken up during this time, let him play a little, give him a little treat and then take him back to bed.

## PUPPY PROOFING

Puppies are hard to keep track of; they are always on the go and often at a faster pace than we can keep up with. One way to keep them safe is by puppy proofing

*Golden Retrievers love digging, especially when young.*

our homes. Ensuring a safe environment need not be expensive and can be done in many ways.

The garden must be secure so your puppy cannot escape. Fencing should be at least 4.5ft high and any gaps should be blocked up with something solid, as most dogs are able to squeeze themselves through tiny gaps in a hedge or fence. Any toxic plants should be removed or placed out of reach, and the same goes for any items and objects that may cause harm to your puppy or dog. If you are very proud of your lawn or planting, fencing an area off exclusively for your dog is worthwhile; urine will damage the grass but also bear in mind that Goldens love to dig and most puppies will nibble on plants.

Inside the house, any valuables that you do not want to risk being chewed should be put away. Make sure your puppy cannot reach any hazardous items, such as electrical wiring (TV, washing machine, fridge, etc.), and move anything that can be pulled down, such as long curtains and house plants.

Giving free run of your house to your new addition opens up a world of possibilities for him, and you may come home to find items have been chewed and he has toileted on a new rug. Confining your puppy to safe areas in the home can help with house training; it can also reduce the amount of trouble your puppy can get himself into and ensures that boundaries are set – for instance, if you do not want your puppy going upstairs, or on carpeted areas.

Stair gates are a popular choice to confine a puppy or dog to a room. However, when choosing a stair or baby gate, ensure your puppy cannot fit his head through the gap. The gate should fit tightly in the allocated gap and secure easily so if your puppy jumps up at it, it will not move and cause any harm.

*Golden puppies love to chew during teething, especially enjoying things that can be ripped up.*

Puppy pens are a popular choice for those who want an alternative to the crate, or who are slowly removing the crate and introducing their puppy to more freedom within the home. Puppy pens should be heavy enough that your puppy cannot move it around when jumping up against the side and, as with the crate, the wires should be at a safe width so his jaws and legs cannot get caught.

**Top Tip**

To prevent mishaps, do not let your puppy/dog have the full run of the house, especially if he is a chewer. Cornering off areas and crate training are both excellent solutions until your puppy/dog is completely trustworthy in the house. Cornering off areas or limiting the areas in the house to which the dog has access can be a permanent decision. For instance, it is far better for your dog to be limited to the kitchen every time he is left alone than given the full run of the house.

## ROUTINE

Puppies thrive on a routine as it provides them with stability and some sort of order, and this is essential for a young puppy settling into a new home. As well as being beneficial to your puppy, it will also enable you to lay down rules and boundaries that accommodate your own routine.

It is best to try to get your puppy into a basic routine, such as having a set feeding time, as soon as he arrives; not only will it help him settle into his new home quickly, but it will make the training process easier as routine means repetition. Find out from the breeder (or wherever your puppy came from) what his current routine is so you can plan around the times when your puppy may be expecting certain things to happen. For instance, if your puppy was used to being let out around midnight for his last toilet and then did not get up again until 5–6am, you can prepare for that to continue. Puppies have weak bladders and need to go out every time they wake up and roughly every two hours when they are awake during the day. As a general rule, puppies sleep for longer at night if they are awake for longer during the day, but puppies do need a lot of sleep, with many only being awake for about six to eight hours each day until they are about six months old. That does not mean that every puppy will sleep for that length of time, however, but having a daily routine will help your puppy settle into regular sleeping patterns.

As a guide, here is an example of a routine suitable for a puppy:

7–8am: wake up and straight outside to toilet
8.30am: breakfast
9am: toilet break
9.30–10am: playtime with some training
10.30am: socialization, then allow him to sleep
11.30am–12 noon: when he wakes naturally, take him outside straight away to toilet
12–1pm: lunch (puppy's second meal)
1.30–2pm: toilet break followed by some light training/playing
3pm: toilet break then allow him to rest
5–5.30pm: toilet break and dinner (puppy's third meal)

5.30–6pm: toilet break and some play/interaction time
6.30–7pm: rest (when you are cooking your own dinner, let your puppy go off to rest, rather than watching you cook, as this can lead to begging for food)
8pm: toilet break followed by a good play session to really tire him out
9pm: bedtime treat (or puppy's last meal when on four meals a day)
10pm: last toilet break of the day and to bed.

This is a guide only and you can, of course, adapt times and events to suit you. Even with the very best efforts, sometimes routines cannot be maintained every day. The routine for your puppy should be flexible so you can carry out your own activities, but bear in mind that too much flexibility may set you back a few steps in training. For example, if you do not let your puppy out to toilet every couple of hours, he is more likely to relieve himself in the house, making house training more difficult in the long run.

## PLAYING

Puppies love to play, and it is their exuberant play that makes them so endearing. There are different types of puppy play; the most common is social play, which involves interacting with you, another dog or even another animal. Social play involves play biting, pawing and barking and/or growling (not to be mistaken for aggression) and can be initiated by the puppy pawing,

*Give your puppy lots of items he can chew and play with.*

*Puppies will often find items they want to play with themselves.*

bowing (where the puppy's front legs stretch out in front, leaving their bottom in the air), leaping, barking, dropping toys in front of you and, if the playmate is a well-known friend, initial play biting. Self-directed play is thought to be a substitute for when a playmate isn't available, and often involves tail chasing. Object play involves interacting with an object, such as a toy, which can be chased, grabbed and chewed or, in the case of the Golden Retriever, picked up and delivered.

Growling during play is completely normal, but puppies (and older dogs) can sometimes get so wound up during play that it turns into bullying. If playmates, or you, stop enjoying the game because it has perhaps become too rough, it is important to stop the play session and let your puppy calm down. This teaches

your puppy what is and isn't acceptable behaviour and how to interact with others.

Ensuring your puppy has enough playtime each day will reduce his need to entertain himself, which often leads to unfortunate naughty behaviour such as chewing furniture. Puppies need to play every day to develop both physically and mentally; it helps to keep them fit and healthy, uses energy, boosts confidence and creates that special bond between man and dog. When playing with your puppy, introduce the toys he is allowed to play with so he learns to play with the right things when he doesn't have human contact.

There are divided opinions about why puppies play. It may be that playing teaches the survival skills needed for life in the wild. This is based on the way puppies grab and play bite, especially around the neck, stalk and pounce and pin down other puppies or dogs, but it doesn't explain why older dogs enjoy playing, who would already have developed those skills in the wild. It may be, then, that dogs are highly sociable and just enjoy the interaction that playing provides. Play could be, as the word suggests, an activity which is simply engaged in for the sake of amusement or fun.

## HOUSE TRAINING

House training takes time and patience, but all puppies get there in the end. If there are accidents in the house, try to stay calm. You can expect a few of them; it is perfectly normal as puppies have very weak bladders and, just like children, can have accidents.

Ensure you let your puppy out every time he wakes up from sleeping and regularly throughout the day and night, always giving lots of praise when he does toilet in the right place. Letting your puppy out regularly helps him learn to toilet in the right place and leads to faster house training. It can prove useful to place a command with the correct toileting, such as saying 'go for wee-wee'. With repetition of this, your puppy will learn to toilet on command. Always let your puppy outside when he has just woken up, after playing, after eating or drinking, as soon as you return home after leaving him on his own, and every two to three hours during the day.

Putting paper down on the floor is one way to teach your puppy where he should relieve himself inside the house. Keep the paper in the same place, and praise him for toileting on the paper. Once he gets the hang of it, reduce the amount of paper put down and place it as close to the back door as possible.

Confining your puppy to a fairly small area, such as a crate or playpen with his bed in it, will encourage him to keep it clean. Have paper covering an small area so he has a chance to toilet somewhere other than his bed. The crate must be a safe and enjoyable space for the puppy and not used for punishment.

Do not punish your puppy if he toilets where he is not supposed to, as he will simply learn to do it when you are not looking. The same goes for if they have had an accident while you have been out; puppies live in the moment, so they will have no idea why you are upset with them.

*Let your puppy just watch what is going on around him; he will explore everything in his own time.*

Let your puppy outside if you see him sniffing the floor, walking slowly on wobbly legs, becoming restless or crying, trying to get your attention, going towards the back door, or trying to find a quiet area.

## GOING OUTSIDE

Taking your puppy into the outside world for the first time can sometimes be daunting and confusing as there are often mixed views about when this should be.

Puppies are allowed to interact with other dogs two weeks after their second vaccination, but it is important to get puppies socialized as early as possible. It is perfectly okay to take your puppy into the outside world while holding him in your arms (if he does not wriggle too much). This allows him to sniff around and get used to his surroundings without coming into contact with other dogs. Only when he has full immunity will be he able to go for proper walks and meet unknown dogs.

The first time you take your puppy Golden out for a walk, he may be a little nervous; don't drag him around on a walk, but let him just sit and watch the world go by. Watching a variety of people, cars, other dogs, cyclists and joggers enables puppies to take it all in their stride. If your puppy is not worried by all that is going on around him, and is lunging ahead to see everything, allow him to explore but do not, at this stage, let him gallop up to every person and dog you meet. Your puppy will be more interested in everything around him than you, which is normal. Take some toys and treats with you so you can get his attention.

After the initial outing, take it steady on the next walks to build up his confidence and release some energy. Allow him to explore at his pace, which will help him to recognize local smells and get an understanding of what is around him. The first walks should only last about ten minutes, building up the time gradually to twenty minutes. It is often tempting to want to walk a Golden puppy until he is so exhausted he will sleep when you take him home, but remember that Golden Retrievers are prone to hip dysplasia and too much exercise at a young age can increase the risk of this disease. If, when you return home, your puppy is

still full of energy, play a game with him instead or give him some food (walking before breakfast or dinner), which will help him settle.

## SOCIALIZING: FOR YOUNG PUPPIES

Socialization for young puppies is vital. During this process puppies learn about themselves, other dogs and species, and develop their personality. Many behavioural problems that surface as your puppy gets older are due to a lack of socialization as a puppy. The most important socialization period for dogs is between three and sixteen weeks of age, and it is essential that during this time your puppy is exposed to as many

*Expose your puppy to all sorts of situations to get him used to his environment.*

different situations as possible. At the same time it is important not to overload him with too many new experiences, especially ones that may cause anxiety. As a guide, aim for one new experience a day so there is a gradual learning curve.

Before your puppy is fully vaccinated, it is worth carrying him to new places so that he can start to see some of his new world. It is not advisable to let your puppy have full access to most public spaces until at least one week after the first vaccination. If possible, try to socialize your puppy in your house and garden with other puppies and vaccinated dogs, and begin early handling and grooming by all the members of the family and visitors to your home. Puppies are like beacons and can attract people to come and say hello, which should be encouraged to ensure your puppy does not become fearful of unknown people.

Socialization exposure, otherwise known as habituation, is the process whereby the puppy becomes accustomed to his environment, its sounds, smells, sights and goings-on.

Here are some suggestions for situations you should familiarize your young puppy with so that he isn't frightened of them when he is older:

- travelling in a car
- seeing large vehicles such as trucks or tractors
- visiting other people's houses
- hearing loud laughter and clapping
- seeing visitors arrive and leave your house
- hearing the television/radio/telephone and other household appliances, such as the washing machine and vacuum cleaner
- meeting another puppy
- meeting an adult dog
- meeting other animals such as cats, rabbits and horses
- meeting children unknown to them
- meeting people with objects such as pushchairs, umbrellas and high visibility clothing.

## PUPPY PARTIES

Puppy parties are a great opportunity for your young puppy to socialize with other dogs of a similar age in a safe and fun environment. Even if your puppy lives with an older dog, he will still benefit from attending a puppy party, which is normally run at a veterinary surgery. Puppy parties also normally include a tour of the surgery, with a veterinary nurse covering aspects of dog care. Attending one of these parties can provide you with an opportunity to ask any questions and get to know your surgery before your puppy needs an appointment.

# CHAPTER 6

# LEARNING THE ROPES

## GREAT EXPECTATIONS

Many owners, often subconsciously, expect too much from young puppies or new dogs in the house. They are expected to learn house rules and obedience overnight and quite often get themselves into a lot of trouble for breaking these rules. Dogs never behave in real life like they do in films or television shows or even dog-training programmes! Real life, after all, does not get edited and there will be good days and bad days when it comes to training.

It is important to remember that dogs are not programmed to know what we want them to do. They need guidance. Too often puppies are punished for what is seen as bad behaviour, rather than being trained to understand what we would like them to do.

Puppies require firm but fair handling and lots of love and affection. Training does not happen overnight

*Try not to expect too much from a young puppy and remember that he learns what you teach.*

and it can sometimes take several months before you start seeing results you are truly happy with. Golden puppies need understanding, persistence and lots of patience.

## WHEN TO TRAIN

Training your puppy or new dog begins the moment you collect him. Every time you stroke him, give him a treat or play with him, you are training him. You are teaching him that you provide food, safety and fun. He will begin to trust you, respect you and listen to you.

The main trick in training a puppy is learning how to keep their concentration. Every time your puppy does a correct action he should be rewarded with praise and/ or a treat. Training should be done in short periods to prevent boredom, and there needs to be lots patience, lots of practice and lots of persistence.

*Allow your puppy plenty of breaks during training and let him sleep when he wants to.*

## PUPPY CLASSES

Puppy classes provide socialization with other puppies of a similar age, where they can interact in a safe, enclosed environment. Classes should cover basic commands such as sit, lie down, stay, walk to heel and recall, with most training classes doing far more than that. Puppy classes help to build up a puppy's confidence around other dogs and people, as well as

learning to listen despite other distractions. They also allow for some uninterrupted time together with your puppy.

When you are looking for suitable puppy classes, do research the group or trainer you are interested in. Some dog trainers run a set course, so everyone joins at the same stage of training and develops at a similar level. Others run rolling courses, where people join at any point and attend weekly or bi-weekly. Most puppy classes cost £5–£10 an hour.

Before booking a puppy class, make sure the dog trainer's training style is suitable to your needs; if you are uncertain, ask if you can watch a puppy class before attending. Positive reinforcement works well with Goldens, because they naturally want to please and will do almost anything for a treat.

Whether you are an experienced dog owner or a first-timer, puppy classes bring a multitude of benefits from attending and, you never know, you may learn something new.

## PLAY BITING

Young puppies are notorious for biting hands, and those sharp puppy teeth can be very painful. But rest assured this is a very normal thing; it doesn't mean that your pup is aggressive, just that he/she is young. If you watch a litter of puppies playing, you'll see them biting one another all the time. The problem is that they often mistake our hands, clothes and ankles for their littermates.

How do we teach the pup not to do this to us? Puppies may see your hands in the same way they see each other's jaws, so don't wave your hands around the pup's face and only use your hands for soft, gentle petting. Don't play games where you and the puppy chase and grab at each other. Play with lots of toys: you can play tug-of-war, fetch and learning games. Make sure the puppy is getting enough exercise: about forty minutes of play a day. This will vary according to the age of your puppy, so base it on how quickly your puppy tires.

Puppies love to play; it is what they live for. So the worst thing that could happen to them is the end of playtime. So if you immediately bring playtime to an

*Even older dogs can be subject to puppy play biting.*

end when they bite you, the rule becomes 'All fun and games end when puppy teeth touch human skin.'

Puppies bite because it's fun, it's their way of playing, and it gains them attention. If you're playing with your puppy and his teeth touch you, yelp loudly and shrilly like a hurt puppy. (If this makes him more excited, or if you're someone who really can't do this, cry out as if he's really hurt you.) For a very short period of time your puppy will stop biting and probably look at you, and if you're lucky you'll have a few seconds before he starts to bite again. In those few seconds disengage yourself from your puppy and very calmly leave him. Stand up and walk away, firmly saying 'No', and do nothing else. If your puppy follows, do not engage with him; do not, for example, pick him up and put him in his crate, as this is still interaction and attention. In short, give him the cold shoulder. You only have to leave him for a little bit (a few seconds or perhaps a minute). He will probably cry or turn his attention to something else. Go back to your puppy but do not make a fuss; just very calmly invite him to say hello. If he goes back to biting immediately, repeat the process (yelp and walk away); it may take a few attempts for your puppy to catch on to

what you are teaching him. The most important thing is to be consistent, as consistency is how puppies learn.

If your puppy is extremely excitable and the cold shoulder technique is not effective, I find 'acting like a dog' works extremely well. Many adult dogs interact with puppies differently from how they interact with adult dogs. They are very calm and lenient with rough play, staying very still and calm when the puppy becomes too rough, or slowly moving away or turning their face away. Even with persistent puppies, most dogs will just remove themselves. Bear in mind, however, that it is far easier for a dog to tolerate puppy biting, because their skin is thicker and tougher than our own. But if you can tolerate soft puppy biting, imitate how an adult dog would behave by not interacting or encouraging them.

Make sure that your puppy is getting lots of praise and attention when he is playing well and gently. Puppies sometimes learn to bite you to get your attention, so make sure that they are rewarded with attention when they're being good, not when they're being naughty. To a puppy, any attention, even scolding, is better than none.

If the biting is very hard and damaging your skin, you

might also want to spray the backs of your hands or your clothes with a chew-deterrent spray, so when your puppy's mouth clamps onto your skin he gets a nasty taste (or, if they like it, they will lick your skin, which is teaching them a soft mouth). When your puppy backs off from biting the nasty taste or licks it, praise him. Only spray the backs of your hands: you don't want your puppy to shy away from your touch if he doesn't like the taste.

Don't forget that whenever you are interacting with a puppy, you are teaching him which actions have good consequences and which ones don't, so always have a treat ready to reward the types of behaviour you want to encourage.

When your puppy starts to respond to the sit and down commands, you can use them to calm him down when he starts forgetting himself and using his mouth too hard.

A note about children: young children and young puppies must always be supervised when they are together. The fast, unpredictable movements of chil-

**Top Tip**

Make sure your puppy is getting enough rest. Sometimes, when puppies end up over-stimulated, they can react like cranky toddlers. To ensure your puppy gets enough sleep, guide him to his bed or put him away in his crate after he has been awake for several hours, after lots of playtime or a walk. A tired puppy should fall asleep after a few minutes. Even if he does not fall asleep straight away, let him have some quiet time to calm him down again.

dren often excite puppies. When puppies accidentally hurt them (and they almost always will), children tend to scream in a way that excites the puppy further, and often run away or wave their arms about, causing the puppy to want to bite them again. Teach young children to move slowly around dogs so that they don't over-

*Paper is often susceptible to being destroyed.*

stimulate them, and to freeze when the puppy starts to get too excited.

Remember that puppy biting is normal and they all grow out of it eventually. Some puppies mature more quickly than others, but keep the three Ps in mind: Persistence, Practice and Patience.

Teaching your puppy how to have a soft mouth will reduce play biting. To start with, show your puppy that you have a treat for him. Once you have his attention, place the treat in the palm of your hand and close your hand around it. He will be inquisitive and want to find it; he may start by biting or scratching at your hand to get to the treat. Without giving any commands or moving your hand away, allow your puppy to work out for himself what he has to do to get the treat. When he realizes that biting and scratching does not work, he will begin to lick your hand or will totally stop altogether and just watch; at this point you should open your hand and allow him to take the treat. This exercise can be done whenever your puppy is play biting, grabbing hands or being over-exuberant when greeting.

## CHEWING

Most puppies go through the stage of chewing items they ought not to chew. It is not a deliberate action done out of spite, but, just as young children are into everything, so puppies are busy exploring the world around them, only using their mouths rather than hands. Common objects that are chewed are wood and soft furnishings; this is largely due to their construction, in that they are easy to wear down and rip apart, which is quite satisfying for a pup.

Chewing is completely normal for puppies, but it becomes a nuisance when the chewing is directed towards items we do not want chewed, such as furniture, clothing or even hands and feet. The issue of destructive chewing should be tackled before it leads to destruction of items, medical problems or a strain on the enjoyment of owning a puppy.

The following steps can be implemented to reduce any destructive or unwanted chewing. Provide suitable items for your puppy to chew. Bear in mind that puppies chew more often when they are teething as their gums become irritated and can be quite painful. Chewing relieves that pain and irritation, so providing your puppy with suitable items that can be chewed during this time will help them to relieve any discomfort without the need to destroy any furniture in the process. Nylabones are a good option, as are dental chew sticks, as they help to encourage appropriate chewing and relieve any gum irritation.

Ensure there are no medical issues. Gastrointestinal problems can cause nausea in dogs, which causes chewing or the eating of copious amounts of grass. Nutritional deficiencies can also have the same effect, and often lead to vomiting after chewing and swallowing any objects. Rule out medical problems by visiting your vet and having a puppy health check to ensure there are no underlying issues that could be causing or contributing to persistent chewing. (In contrast, if your puppy is normally a chewer but has stopped completely or gone off his food, looks unwell and is very quiet in his behaviour, he should be taken to the vet.)

Remove temptation. If your puppy is a prolific chewer, always make sure there are no potential dangers for an inquisitive puppy to take an interest in. Put out of reach any medications, household cleaners and chemicals, electrical wiring and toxic plants. If you are unable to move any of these items out of reach, they should be covered up or made inaccessible. Do remove any objects of particular interest to Goldens, who are partial to shoes, socks and children's toys. Do not leave your puppy unsupervised in a room that has not been puppy-proofed, to avoid any damage to either items or puppy.

Encourage good chewing by providing chew toys for your puppy. Each individual puppy will have his own preference, be it a cuddly toy, an old toilet roll, a squeaky ball, a rope, a kong or a rubber toy. Try out lots of different types to see which ones he prefers. Be careful to select the right size: your puppy should be able to pick up and carry the toy, but it should not be so small that it cannot be seen when held in his mouth. Be careful with any food chews, such as raw hide, as these can splinter and be chewed into small pieces that can get lodged in the oesophagus if swallowed. It is recommended that a puppy given a raw hide or similar chew should be supervised and any small pieces removed. Do not give your puppy inappropriate toys such as old shoes, because he will not know the difference between an old shoe and a new one.

Play with your puppy: chewing is often done out of boredom. If you play lots with your puppy, he will be more tired and less inclined to occupy himself. Spend time playing with him and provide regular exercise, even if it's just a little walk around the garden and five minutes of throwing out a ball. This time together not only reinforces the human–dog bond, but will provide the stimulation and interaction your puppy craves after leaving his litter mates. If energy is spent on playtime, there will be less of it to spend chewing.

Do not allow your puppy to chew inappropriate items. Following the above suggestions will help minimize the amount of chewing of inappropriate items, but if you do catch your puppy chewing something that he shouldn't, say a firm 'no' and take the item away (if possible) and replace it with an item that he *can* chew on. When he chews on the correct item, give him lots of praise. Gradually your puppy will learn which items are for chewing and which not. Deterrent sprays such as bitter apple can be applied to objects that are chewed frequently; the unpleasant taste can deter chewing, and make the object less desirable.

Try not to lose your patience with a chewing puppy. In many cases it's a phase that doesn't last too long and it can be dealt with in the right circumstances. If you will be out of the house for long periods of time,

*Puppies love to steal items; even an old glove makes an interesting toy.*

ensure your puppy is placed in a crate so he cannot develop any bad chewing habits.

## BEING LEFT ALONE

Puppies and dogs can become very distressed when left on their own, even if just for a short period, and separation anxiety is one of the biggest problems for many owners. Separation anxiety is the term used for a dog that becomes distressed when left alone, and this distress is displayed through being destructive, barking, howling, chewing, digging, toileting indoors, pacing or even trying to escape.

If you come home and find your house in disrepair time after time, the chances are your dog has separation anxiety. When you are about to leave, does he start to drool, pace, bark or obsessively follow you around? These could be signs that your dog is becoming distressed. Even minor distress should be resolved before it develops and manifests into destruction in the house, normally through chewing, especially around doors or windows.

Do not punish your dog if you come home and find he has toileted in the house or chewed anything. Anxiety is a distress response, and matters can only be made worse if you shout at your dog on your return; dogs live in the moment and will not understand that your irritation is linked to something that may have happened hours earlier. Many people say, 'My dog knows because he has a guilty look on his face', or 'He sulks when I return home', but in fact these dogs are purely reacting to the owner's body language and tone of voice on their return. If you punish your dog when he is doing nothing, you will provoke the same fearful reaction, and it does not solve the problem to get angry after the misdemeanour has been committed.

If you have an older dog who is urinating when left alone, do not rule out medical problems. Older dogs may be incontinent, so it worth making a trip to the vet before jumping to any conclusions. Puppies also cannot control their bladders and will need to be let out more regularly. If you have a young dog who is destructive when left alone, this could be down to boredom. All dogs need mental stimulation, and this is especially true of young Goldens, who are easily bored and will

*Gates allow you to restrict where your dog is allowed when you are out.*

find other ways to entertain themselves, which is a separate matter altogether.

If you are uncertain whether your dog suffers from separation anxiety, you can purchase cameras to place in the room where the dog is and watch how he behaves when alone. A cheaper alternative is to ask your neighbours whether they can hear any excessive barking, howling or crying. If the dog does not notice you, you can peek through the windows to see how the dog is after you leave and before you go back inside.

All dogs can experience separation anxiety, but it is especially common in dogs that have been rescued, or have lost a loved one, possibly through death or moving away. A change in ownership can bring on anxiety; this is especially seen in puppies in a new home, who will cry during the night or when left alone. It will also occur if there is a change in schedule, such as moving house, children going to school, or someone who normally works from home changing to an office-based job.

Your dog needs to learn that it is okay to be left alone, and that you will return. This requires training and a change in habit to show your dog that the situation is not stressful. It is best done gradually if possible, and this is where crate training comes in very handy if you have a crate, puppy pen or secure room to leave your dog in. If your dog is left in the kitchen, using a baby gate across the doorway will prevent him from having the run of the house but also allows him to see out, rather than feeling trapped behind a closed door.

To begin the process, give your dog a tasty treat or a favourite toy that he can munch on or play with for some time and then, without any fuss, leave the room for a couple of minutes and then return while he is still happily occupied. Once your dog is happy to be left like this, repeat the process again without the treat; just

**Top Tip**

Remember that dogs must not be left for long periods of time. If you do go out for more than four to five hours, have someone let your dog out for you. It is cruel to expect your dog to not relieve himself for more than four hours and, being a pack animal, he will become lonely if left for a long time.

   If you do take your dog out with you, never leave him in a car, especially during the summer months, as the outcome can be fatal. Dogs die in hot cars because they cannot cool themselves down by sweating. Goldens have a very thick coat, so I would not recommend leaving your dog in a conservatory or any hot room during the summer.

walk out of the room and return a few minutes later. Do not make a fuss of your dog while you are leaving or entering the room; instead think of it as completely normal practice. As hard as it is, do not say goodbye or give cuddles and kisses; this only exacerbates the problem and makes it a 'big deal' for the dog rather than normal everyday life.

   The next stage is to plan short absences. The best time to leave your dog is after exercise as he will naturally be more tired and more likely to sleep while you are away. Start by leaving the house for just a few minutes and return to your dog when he is calm. Once you know your dog is happy to be left for a short period,

you can build the time up gradually to thirty minutes, then an hour, and so on.

   Do not return to your dog if he starts to howl, cry or bark, or it can become his way of calling you back – in response to their call you magically appear. If your dog is prone to barking in your absence, it could be that you only leave the room or house for a minute, but you must return to him before he begins barking. Dogs do not have the same concept of time as humans so you can build up the absent time, but it must be a gradual process.

   If your dog has severe separation anxiety and begins showing signs of stress before you even leave, note

*Here a dog waits patiently at the gate.*

*A Golden Retriever and a Border Terrier playing happily.*

what is triggering the problem. Does your dog react to certain actions such as you picking up car keys or putting a coat on? Does he react when he is placed in a certain room? Does he respond when you say 'goodbye'? Once you are aware of exactly what is triggering his reactions, you can begin undoing the links that those actions cause. All those tell-tale signs that show your dog you are about to leave need to be seen as normal activity that he does not need to stress about. Begin by picking up your keys (or whatever item causes signs of stress), carry them around with you and then put them back down again without leaving the house. The same applies if your dog reacts to you putting on a coat; put it on without going anywhere, and then take it off again. This needs to be done on a daily basis to desensitize your dog to certain actions. He will learn that picking up the keys does not necessarily mean you will leave. Once you have taken away the stress cues, he will relax. When he no longer reacts to you picking up the keys, you can begin to leave him for a few minutes at a time, following the stages mentioned above.

Puppies should not be left alone for more than three hours, and adult dogs no more than five hours. Not only are you leaving your dog alone, but you are preventing him from relieving himself. If you cannot be back for your dog within five hours of leaving, arrange for someone to come in and let him out.

## SOCIALIZATION: FOR AN OLDER PUPPY

The experiences your puppy has in the first year of his life will make all the difference to the development of his character and temperament for the future. Taking the time to socialize your puppy properly will help produce a friendly, outgoing Golden who enjoys the company of other people and dogs, can be taken anywhere and be placed in every situation with confidence, and generally lives a happy life. It is important that puppies experience pleasant encounters with people of all ages and with different species of animals. From early puppyhood they should also be exposed to a wide range of environments and events. As your puppy develops, his socialization should develop too.

Lack of socialization can lead to a fearful and emotionally unbalanced dog, and dogs with such traits are more unpredictable in their behaviour and more likely to bite in certain situations.

Developing socialization can be balanced with how your older puppy reacts to situations. Be wary still not to overwhelm him, but you can start introducing him to more 'stressful' environments; at large events such as country fairs, for example, there will be lots of people, animals, machinery and loud noises. Judge your puppy's reaction to see whether he is able to cope with it, and never force him into situations where he is fearful. You can begin to prepare him for things like Bonfire Night by playing firework noises; to begin with keep the volume low and behave as if the noise is entirely normal, gradually increasing the sound until he is accustomed to it. This method can be used with any noises that are typically frightening for dogs.

## BAD EXPERIENCES

If your puppy has an experience which has a negative effect in that it frightens him, try not to coo over or pander to him. Instead, act normally as this will condition your puppy to accept scary situations and show him that there is nothing to be afraid of. Cuddling up to your puppy will have the opposite effect as he will not know you are trying to comfort him and this 'rewarding' reaction from you only encourages the frightened behaviour in your puppy.

If there are loud noises, such as fireworks going off, go about your normal business but have the radio or television volume turned up slightly higher than normal to dull the frightening sounds. Do not leave your puppy alone during his first Bonfire Night or New Year's Eve, when fireworks are likely to be set off, as being left alone during stressful times is often when these fears erupt.

## STRESSFUL SITUATIONS

Dogs can suffer from stress as much as you or I, and stressful situations can bring on anxiety and fear. Stress can be triggered by a bad experience, which leads to anxious behaviour in certain situations. The most common situations which bring on anxiety are:

- Separation anxiety: normally brought on by being left alone for long periods of time without the proper training;
- Noise anxiety: a fear of loud or unexpected noises such as fireworks or thunder;
- Travel anxiety: movement can cause travel sickness, which in turns become a stressful situation for a dog, especially for young puppies who haven't yet been exposed to short, frequent journeys;
- Lead anxiety: this type of anxiety is common in dogs who have had a bad experience with another dog when on the lead. When a dog feels trapped (as he is on a lead), and cannot flee away from danger, his fear is likely to manifest itself as aggression, which can lead to him snapping at other dogs to warn them away.

The signs of stress can differ from dog to dog, but the most common are:

- excessive panting
- constant barking

*Loud or unexpected noises can worry dogs; look at their body language to see how they feel.*

- biting feet
- excessive licking
- chewing
- toileting
- cowering and other submissive body signals
- aggression.

If your dog is showing any of these signs, the chances are he is suffering from a level of anxiety. It is quite easy to get angry with your dog, especially if he is being noisy or destructive in the home, but this is counter-productive, as it does not address the problem and can increase the dog's uncertainty.

To combat stress, try one or more of the following techniques.

Get your dog's attention with a favourite treat or toy, asking for easy commands such as sit and lie down, and rewarding when the commands are followed. Desensitizing your dog to certain situations can help him forget about what is going on around him and focus on you. In doing so, he will calm down and begin to associate the stressful situation with stimulation from you and a pleasant experience. It also allows him to stay in control rather than panic and focus solely on the stressful situation. This technique is best for loud and unexpected noises and lead anxiety.

Keeping everything calm can help your dog to calm down in a stressful situation, as can changing your environment. For example, changing the way you travel in your car can reduce travel anxiety; if you normally have the radio on, turn it off when your dog is with you. Or, if you have a very quiet car, put the music on to distract your dog. Changing your behaviour when out on a walk will do wonders for your dog too. If you become nervous every time you come across another dog, your dog will become nervous too, so stay in control and give yourself enough distance from the other dog to calm your nerves. Changing your own behaviour can actually bring down your dog's stress levels. Golden Retrievers are very sensitive to their owner's moods and if they sense you are becoming anxious or stressed, they will reflect it. This technique is best for travel and lead anxiety and coping with loud noises.

There are many calming products and medications on the market that assist in soothing our dogs. They can come in many forms, ranging from aerosols that are sprayed in the house, releasing a pheromone, to tablets for motion sickness or tablets containing a mild seda-tive. It is not clear how well these products work but even if they do they will only mask the problem and not resolve it. Calming products are best kept for extremely stressful situations where your dog is in danger of hurt-ing himself or others because of his behaviour. Always speak to your vet before using any product on your dog to solve anxiety issues.

A relatively new concept is the thundershirt: a close-fitting top with straps that wrap around your dog's torso and provides light pressure on his body. This pressure can have a calming effect during stressful situations that bring on anxiety. The thundershirt should be used with other training methods to resolve any anxiety behaviour, and simply placing one on your dog will not result in an instantly calm dog. The thundershirt is best used for separation anxiety and coping with loud noises.

# CHAPTER 7

# TRAINING

## COMMUNICATING

Communication with your dog lasts a lifetime. It starts from the moment you select your puppy, until the sad day when he passes away. It comes in many different forms and works both ways: you communicating with your dog and your dog with you.

We communicate mostly through voice; we give commands and often talk to our dogs. Our dogs, however, communicate mostly through body language. The most obvious form of body language is the joyous wag of your Golden's tail to signify happiness, excitement and interest.

To connect fully with our dogs we must learn to communicate with them in every form, through our voice, body language and facial expressions, and in turn we must listen to our dog's complex communication through his voice, body language and facial expressions.

## WHAT THE DOG'S VOICE MEANS

Dogs talk to us in a variety of ways, through a range of whimpers, whines, barks, howls, murmurs, growls and sighs that indicate what he is trying to say. Some whines are pleading, others attention seeking; some barks may be warnings, others an invitation to play; and howls may be a recall for their owner or a response to an intense noise. Pay attention to your Golden and get to know his vocalization so you can learn what each one may mean.

## WHAT THE DOG'S FACIAL EXPRESSION MEANS

Goldens have the most irresistible faces in the dog world, with their soft expression and big dark eyes; it is very easy to give in to their requests when they give you 'the puppy-dog look'. Beyond the doe-eyed look

*An owner gives the sit command with a hand signal.*

*The Golden Retriever has a very expressive look.*

(which is often a plea for food), our dogs use many facial expressions to communicate with us. Giving eye-to-eye contact, looking away, looking out of the corner of their eye, a hard stare or a flash of the whites of the eye are all ways in which our dogs communicate with us and the world around them.

Where your dog looks, coupled with the direction of his ears and the way he is holding his mouth, can tell you more about how he is feeling than his voice can. These are sometimes subtle and secretive expressions not necessarily directed at you or anyone else but simply a reflection of his emotion.

## WHAT THE DOG'S BODY LANGUAGE MEANS

Your dog can use the whole of his body in a variety of ways to communicate with you. The position of the tail is an obvious indicator of your dog's mood; it can be wagged, tucked up tight underneath the body, held stiffly, relaxed or nervously twitched.

Gestures can be large, such as dogs rolling over in submission, crouching down, or making themselves look as big as possible by standing upright and raising the hackles (the hair found along the back, between the shoulders and hips). Gestures can also be smaller, such as hanging the head a little lower than normal or walking more slowly.

The more you watch your dog, the more you will discover the breadth of combinations he uses to communicate with you. Learn to understand him; there is something deeply satisfying about being able to understand your dog through his choices of language.

## THE SENSES

You may notice that your Golden spends a fair amount of walks with his nose to the ground. Dogs interpret the world around them through their incredible sense of smell, which has up to 300 million sense receptors. As frustrating as it may be to be constantly having to stop and wait while your dog sniffs what seems like every blade of grass, he is actually taking in everything around him. It is because of their incredible

*A very relaxed Golden enjoys snuggling up and snoozing.*

sense of smell that dogs know, if they get lost, how to find their way home.

Dogs take in scent through short inhaled sniffing, which leaves behind a scent to be read while the air is inhaled. A wet nose also helps them smell by capturing scent particles. A dog who is excessively panting reduces his sense of smell as the air intake is through the mouth to cool the body down from overheating.

It was once believed that dogs saw only in black and white. But since then studies have shown that dogs can see a number of colours, predominantly shades of blue, yellow and grey. It is true that dogs can see images on the television, but as their resolution ability is higher than that of humans, the images are likely to appear to them as strobe lighting does to us. Some breeds of dog, especially sight hounds, have better vision than others and can see much further; the Golden Retriever's overall vision is not great in comparison but they do still have better low-light vision than humans do.

Puppies are born deaf and do not start to hear until they are on average two to three weeks old. Once their hearing has developed, they can hear sounds at more than four times greater distances than a human can, and can hear higher-pitched sounds. There are eighteen muscles in a dog's ears, meaning they can move

their ears around at different angles. Golden Retrievers, with their floppy ears, cannot move their ears like a radar on their head, but they can still move them around to assist with hearing. Ears pricked forwards show the dog is interested and listening, which for a Golden is normally when food is available. Ears down and flat against the head often indicate nervousness, fear or submission. There are many combinations of ear movement, with each position having a separate meaning, and some that are unique to your dog.

As your dog ages, he may, as some humans do, lose his vision and his ability to hear certain frequencies. It is important to be mindful of this as he ages, and if necessary alter your own behaviour and ways to communicate with your dog. For instance, you can teach your dog hand signals for commands, rather than using voice commands.

Watching your dog is a great way of learning and picking up on his communication; the more you watch, the more you learn.

## REWARDS

Positive reinforcement has seen many benefits in training dogs; most importantly, it makes training enjoyable

*The Golden Retriever has an incredible sense of hearing.*

*Toys can be an effective treat.*

for both owner and dog. The key to positive reinforcement is that you reward the good behaviour; Golden Retrievers naturally want to please and will respond with enthusiasm to positivity (and a treat). Timing is vital when it comes to giving the reward; it must be given instantly after the good behaviour so the two are linked together in the dog's mind, making training more efficient.

Treats are the most common form of positive reinforcement. They are convenient, relatively clean and normally the perfect motivation for Goldens. They should be used sparingly, though, and if a lot of treats are used in a particular training session, then the dog's next meal should be reduced or his weight may start to creep up. There are multiple options for treats, dog biscuits being the most obvious, but small pieces of

cooked meat such as chicken also make a very tasty alternative.

Games are a fun way to reward, and any Golden Retriever will relish going to retrieve a toy after training. You can initiate playtime when your dog has behaved well. For instance, give the 'sit' command and when your dog has obeyed, throw the toy out for retrieving. You can then ask your dog to 'leave it' or 'lie down' (or any other command), and then throw the toy again, so your dog is working and learning commands in reward for the toy. Tug-of-war is the most instant reward game and can be just as effective.

Attention is also a reward. Most Goldens love having our undivided attention, whether this is in the form of a pat on the head or having your arms wrapped around them. Attention can be brought into training by stroking your dog and telling him he's a 'good boy', after he has carried out the command asked for. Your dog will learn that certain behaviour gets your attention and affection.

## DISCIPLINE

Disciplining your dog is important in that it teaches him what behaviour is unacceptable. If used alongside positive reinforcement, your dog will clearly be able to see the difference between acceptable and unacceptable behaviour. But discipline should not be confused with punishment, which is carried out negatively and normally in anger. If correctly carried out, discipline can help the training process.

Never shout at or hit your dog. He will only learn from this to be afraid of you and this can destroy trust. Remember that dogs do not behave in a certain way out of spite and they do not understand long lectures. They must be treated as dogs where training and discipline is concerned.

When you tell your dog 'no', if he is doing something you do not want him to do, do not say his name as well. His name should be used for positive reinforcement and as a way to get his attention. Be firm and assertive (but not angry) when you say 'no', and you should only need to say it once. Your tone of voice and your body language are key in delivering the correct message in showing your displeasure at his behaviour, and will depict leadership. If you find yourself getting angry, walk away for a few minutes, or have a cup of tea and only return when you have calmed down.

**CHAPTER 8**

# BASIC COMMANDS

## SIT

Most dogs learn how to sit from a very young age and do it automatically with little intervention. As we are much taller than them, when we stand over our dogs they will crane their necks back to look up at us, and it is more comfortable for them to go into the sit position than to keep standing and looking up at us. You can couple this natural action with a treat in your hand, holding it slightly above the dog's head, and the moment he sits, reward him instantly.

When your dog goes into a comfortable sit position, say the command 'sit'. By training the action first and then putting a command to that action, your dog will learn not to ignore a command. If you give a command before the dog has learnt what the word means, it will only cause confusion and frustration for both of you.

## LIE DOWN

To ask your dog to lie down, first face him head on and put him into a sit. Hold a treat very close to his face, almost within reaching distance, and then move it from their nose down towards their front feet, creat-ing a swan-like arch in the dog's neck. As he bends his neck down for the treat, bring it towards you. This will encourage your dog to extend his neck and bring his shoulders down, which will naturally develop into a 'lie down'. Reward instantly.

*Training should continue throughout your dog's life, not just in puppyhood.*

**Top Tip**

Allowing your dog to work out what to do to get a reward is enjoyable for him. It also encourages brain activity and heightens his intelligence. Forcing your dog to obey a command (such as pushing his bottom down into sit) often leads to stubbornness and ultimately a dog who does not listen. Your dog should be able to respond to all commands when he is out of reach and off the lead, so it is best to train him that way from the start rather than allowing bad habits to creep in.

*Hold the treat close to the floor to encourage a 'lie down'.*

If your dog stands up when the treat is brought outwards, try taking it back towards his back feet, either through his legs or to one side; this will cause your dog to flop into a lie down. Again, reward straightaway.

Once your dog gets the idea that lying down results in him getting the treat, he should move into this position more quickly and with ease. When you are achieving a smoother 'lie down' you can begin to incorporate the command you want to use, such as 'down'.

## STAND-UP

The 'stand-up' command is best taught when the dog is lying down. To achieve a 'stand-up', take another treat and bring it out towards you, far enough away that the dog has to stand up and take a step towards you to receive the reward. If you do not take it far enough away he may try to crawl along the floor (a neat party trick if you want to teach them that). As your dog is standing up, give the command, so action and command go hand in hand.

## STAY

To achieve a solid stay, first introduce time and then distance. When first learning this command, dogs can handle staying for a length of time better than staying at a distance.

Begin by placing your dog in either the sit or down position, whichever he holds better. Without giving a reward, stand upright and, keeping your dog's attention, count for a few seconds; while your dog is still engaged and looking at you, reward him.

*Asking for a stay while in the sit position. Start with time and then increase distance.*

Keeping him in the stay position, gradually build up the time until your dog is achieving at least a minute of stay with you in close proximity. Once he can reliably hold his position for between half a minute and a minute, you can begin to incorporate distance.

*To create a solid 'stay with distance', just take a few steps away to begin with.*

Begin by telling your dog to stay and then take one small step away from him; after a few seconds (or however long you feel comfortable with), return to your dog and reward him. Always return to your dog before he stands up as it will help to teach a firm 'stay'. If you reward your dog when he is standing up it will encourage him to break the 'stay' command, and come and retrieve his treat when it suits him.

Build up the distance little by little, taking a few steps away and returning. When teaching stay, I always ask that owners return to their dogs while they are learning the command. If you ask for a 'recall' from a 'stay', the dog will start to anticipate the next command in sequence, and no matter what you say, even if it is not 'come', they will recall anyway because dogs learn by repetition.

Once they are staying in place while you walk away and return, include some time control; take a few steps away, wait for a minute and then return and reward. You can build up as much distance and time with your dog as you would like.

## WALKING ON THE LEAD

To begin training your dog to walk nicely on the lead, start with the basics; teach him not to walk across you or behind you, but instead at one side. This exercise can be done with both puppies and dogs who pull on the lead. Walking on the lead training can begin as soon as your puppy comes to you; if you are waiting for his vaccinations, you can practise around your house or garden in the meantime.

Dog leads tend to be short, but for training purposes, especially when teaching a dog not to pull, a short lead can have a detrimental effect. Instead, use a long, flat lead. To begin, encourage your dog not to run ahead of you by gently guiding him back with the lead (do not yank or pull him sharply), and reward him with lots of praise and a treat when he is in the right position.

Have your lead in one hand, with your dog on the opposite side to that hand. Hold a treat in the hand nearest the dog, and show it to him. Do not hold the treat too high as this will encourage jumping up. Instead, have it close enough to his face to keep him interested. Guide your dog forward for a few steps, with him walking beside you, and when he is walking nicely, without pulling ahead or back, reward him with the treat and praise. Build the distance up until you can walk comfortably around without having your Golden charging ahead.

Once your dog is happily walking around with you like this, start to move the treat further away from his face; your dog should still be engaging with you and should not revert back to darting around on the lead. If he begins to jump up, sit down or charge ahead, repeat the first steps again.

Soon you will be able to move onto the next stage, where you walk upright with your hands loose by your sides. Remember to relax your arms when walking; if there is any tension in the lead, it will only encourage your dog to pull against you. Keep your dog's attention by rewarding little and often, and when he is striding out next to you without pulling on the lead you can begin to incorporate the word you wish to use to signify walking by your side, such as 'heel'.

*Walking two dogs should be done the same way as walking one dog. It is a matter of personal preference whether to walk with one on either side or both on one side of you.*

### Top Tip

Start as you mean to carry on, so begin asking your dog to walk nicely beside you the moment you leave your house, not just when you reach the park. Goldens are very strong dogs and if not correctly trained to walk on the lead they may use their full strength to drag you along to where they want to go. But they are very intelligent dogs with a natural desire to please, so with lots of practice and patience walking to heel nicely can be accomplished. For the best results, start training walking to heel from a young age and continue the training every time you take your dog on a walk.

Remember to make training fun. Dogs will be more interested in you if you are fun to be with, so play with them when they are getting bored and take regular breaks during a training session. Too much training and not enough play will cause napping behaviour.

If you have a very strong dog, there are head collars available that loop around the dog's head and give you full control. They will not solve the problem, and your dog will probably still pull when not wearing it, but it does provide an instant effect.

# RECALL

Recall is one of the most important commands to teach your dog, especially when you start to let them off the lead and need to call them back.

Young Goldens have a short attention span, so keep the recall simple to start with and work with their natural ability. Start by getting your dog to follow you around; this can be done by walking into another room and encouraging your dog to come to you, simply by calling his name. As he comes towards you, praise him and reward him with a treat and a fuss.

If your dog does not follow you, try not to repeatedly call his name as this will only teach him that it is acceptable to ignore your calls. Instead, make a noise that will interest him; this might be rustling something or tapping on a hard surface or simply making clicking noises, but it must be a noise that is not familiar to him. Since Goldens are naturally inquisitive, he cannot help but want to investigate and he will come to have a look at the source of the noise. When he does come to you, reward him just as if he had come when you called his name the first time.

*Reward your dog every time he returns to you.*

**Top Tip**

Boring walks and lack of interaction may tempt Goldens to run off to play with another dog or to go off to find something more interesting to do. They enjoy social interaction and entertainment, and they like to have a play friend out on walks, so they will quite happily go and seek entertainment elsewhere if it does not come from you. When you are out walking with your dog, play games with him when he is off the lead. You can take a toy or incorporate games like hide and seek or simply run around with him. You will become a lot more interesting to your dog once you start getting involved with him on walks. It will also build a strong friendship and teach him to keep an eye on you if you are unpredictable and fun.

There is an old saying which goes: 'If a dog runs towards you, whistle.' This is an old but effective way of training a dog to recall and means that whenever your dog is coming towards you, you should give the command 'come' or 'here' (or whichever word or command you prefer) or use a whistle. This method of training places a command with an action, which when repeated is learnt effectively through association. If you ask your dog to 'come' before he has learnt what the word means, you will not get the quick response that the command should carry and you will end up with a dog who saunters back to you in his own time.

Goldens have a tendency towards sudden selective hearing when you try to call them back from something they are interested in. This could be another dog, a person, an interesting smell, a dead animal or another animal's faeces. From a very young age, when out on a walk, allow your dog time off the lead. If his recall is a bit hit-and-miss, let him off in a quiet, secure location and practise the recall by including a retrieving game. Throw a toy out for him to retrieve and as he comes back with it, call his name and offer a treat on his return. Goldens work best with positive training

**Top Tip**

Make sure your dog comes all the way up to you when he has been recalled, otherwise he can boomerang off in another direction when he is halfway back. If your dog is prone to being side-tracked, offer him a tasty treat for coming all the way back, hold on to his collar for a few seconds and then allow him to go off and run around again. Some dogs avoid coming back if they know they are going to go back on the lead, so make sure you don't put your dog on the lead every time you recall him.

and getting angry with your dog for not returning can be counter-productive, as he will learn to avoid you in fear of being told off.

If your dog refuses to come to you and tries to lure you into a game by running away, stopping and facing you again, or going into the bow position, walk away from him. Don't go so far that you are out of sight. Most dogs cannot bear being left alone and will naturally follow if they think you are leaving. Of course, this method can only be used if your dog is watching you!

If your dog frequently tries to initiate play with you when out on a walk, he is likely to be telling you that he isn't getting enough playtime or interaction. This type of behaviour can be due to the following:

- routine walks have become boring;

- there is not enough interaction from you during the walk;
- there are no other doggy playfriends around; or
- it is a habit that your dog has learnt (normally tried because it has worked before).

It is important that your dog gets enough interaction on walks, but he must also know when it is not playtime. By walking away from him, you are telling him to listen to you and that you are in control of playtime.

If you have a particularly stubborn dog who will not return to you, keep walking and encourage him to follow (as long as he is not causing a nuisance, and is not in any danger or in a large open space with lots of escape routes). Do not feel tempted to go and get him, or he will expect that from you all the time and it will

*Your Golden should do an enthusiastic recall back to you.*

become a habit. If your dog persists with this trick, go back to training the recall in a quiet and secure location or walk your dog on a long training lead so you can always get him back.

## LEAVE

Golden Retrievers are into everything and will pick up pretty much anything that will fit into their mouth. Teaching the leave command is important for when you need to take something from your dog. It is part of their natural retrieving instinct, so if you make it into a game it can become lots of fun.

To teach the leave command, place an item of value to your dog on the floor, such as a sock or any other item you do not want them to pick up. As he picks it up, show him a treat in your hand. If he is not paying attention, hold it quite close to his face so he can see and smell the treat; he will drop the item he has picked up to take the food, and at this point you should say 'leave'.

**Top Tip**

To get his attention call your dog's name and, with your arms wide open, kneel down to his level; this is much more welcoming and more inviting than being scolded or shouted at before he has even reached you.

Do not ask your dog to sit when he returns to you as you will be rewarding the sit, not the recall. If he starts to recall but detours halfway, make it exciting to catch you up; this can be done by walking backwards, running away or bringing a toy – anything that might spark his interest.

*The drop can be incorporated with retrieve. Ensure your dog drops the item into your hand for a clean handover.*

Here a Golden has laid down with a toy rather than bring it back.

**Top Tip**

Golden Retrievers were bred to retrieve items and there is nothing they love more than being allowed to go and fetch things. The 'leave' command can be easily incorporated into a retrieving exercise; why not teach your dog to collect certain objects, such as keys or slippers, and bring them to you.

The next step is to place the object back on the floor. As he goes to pick it up, say 'leave' firmly, and when he turns back to you, reward him. This can take time to master and it will depend on how highly your dog rates certain objects. If it is turned into a game or a job, the command will soon become much more meaningful to your Golden.

Spraying your dog with water from a water pistol can be an effective way of stopping bad behaviour (such as picking up items he shouldn't or even getting off the sofa) but it can be detrimental to their love of water and their trust in you. Discipline should always be firm but fair and, as Goldens are such soft-natured dogs, a firm voice should be more than enough to get the message across.

Begin training by throwing an item for your dog; when he picks it up, call him back and reward him with a treat when he drops the item to take the treat. Throw the item again, but this time give the command 'fetch the keys', or the name of the item that has been thrown, and then repeat the recall process. If you want your dog to fetch keys, attach something soft to the keys that he can hold in his mouth; hard metal in his mouth will be a deterrent to begin with.

If your dog runs off with an item instead of bringing it to you, try not to chase after him as it soon turns into a game, and your dog will run off with items to get you to play with him. If your dog picks something up and runs off with it, throw out some biscuits to coax him towards you. He will drop what is in his mouth for the treats and as he follows a trail of biscuits he will leave the item behind. At this stage you can call him towards you and distract him with something else to play with, such as a favourite toy. Only go back to the item he so wanted to play with when he is no longer interested in it. That way it will not become an object of high interest just to get your attention, which is often why Goldens steal things like socks and shoes – because it gets an instant reaction.

If the item he has picked up is of high value to him, tempting him with biscuits is unlikely to work; instead, try giving a more tasty reward, such as a strip of cooked chicken or something similar.

Never try to force your dog's mouth open if he has hold of something he is not willing to give up easily; you are more likely to get accidentally bitten if you do.

## RETRIEVE

Training for Golden Retrievers must, in my opinion, include the retrieve. Most Goldens do not need to be taught how to do it; it is their natural instinct after all. But retrieving to command is a great way to channel your dog's natural abilities and give him a job to do. The retrieve (or fetch) can be taught at any age and can be done with any number of objects, such as your slippers, the car keys or even the dog's own lead.

**Top Tip**

This same exercise can be used in any situation where your dog shows interest in something you do not want him to approach, such as dead animals or another animal's faeces. Always carry a supply of extra delicious treats for those just-in-case moments, as even the very best trained dog can get sidetracked if there is something of great interest!

*Ask your Golden to retrieve a toy from water to keep this training exercise fun.*

**Top Tip**

If your dog is reluctant to bring his prize back to you, throw a favourite treat towards him so he leaves the object and goes after the treat. As he takes the treat, recall him all the way and give him lots of praise. If you make a big deal out of taking the object off him, he will become even more reluctant to hand it over. Alternatively he may entice you into a game of chase if he knows you will come after him for the retrieved object, so always ensure he comes back to you and ignore any 'chase me' behaviour.

Special dummies are available for those wanting their dog to be a working dog and retrieve game; they can be purchased in most specialist shops and come in a variety of weights.

To begin training, show your dog the item you want picked up and get him interested in it by encouraging him to play with it. Then throw the object out; your dog will naturally chase after it and as he does, say 'fetch' or 'retrieve'. As he picks up the object, give him the recall command. As he reaches you, ask him to 'leave' and reward him.

## GO TO BED

Teaching your dog to 'go to bed' is an easy way to get him to settle down or stay out of the way for a short period. It should not be used as a form of punishment, but as a nice, safe place for your dog to go to settle down and sleep.

To begin, make your dog's bed comfortable and clean and put some favourite toys and chews in there, in case he does not want to sleep. Throw a biscuit into the bed and as he follows it, say 'on your bed'. Once your dog is in his bed, get him to lie down and stay there for a few minutes and then invite him out. Repeat this process, gradually building up the time, until your dog is happy to go into his bed and settle down.

Eventually you will be able to just point to the bed and give the command without needing the treats. If

*'Go to bed' should not be used as a punishment, but as a command to let your dog settle down.*

you need your dog to go to his bed while you are at home, do not leave him there for hours on end. Goldens are sociable dogs and would rather settle anywhere with you than be left behind.

## STOP BARKING

Persistent barking can be a nuisance, not just to you but to others around you, so training your dog to 'stop barking' is a useful command and removes the need to shout at him.

Remember that dogs will naturally guard their home, so you should expect them to bark if someone comes to the door. Most of us want our dogs to warn us if someone unknown is approaching, but with these simple steps they can alert you and then be quiet.

When your dog barks, walk up to him and get him to sit, and follow up with the 'stop barking' command. Use a calming phrase like 'all right' instead of a reprimand like 'no'. Your dog will respond more quickly if you are giving him a command. Now he has something to concentrate on, he will focus on the command and, even if just for a split second, will stop barking.

The moment he stops barking praise him and reward the good behaviour. If he starts to bark again, ask him to lie down; again, when he stops barking reward him.

By distracting him and teaching him a new command, he will be focused on you, drawing his attention away from whatever was making him bark.

## TEACHING TRICKS

Golden Retrievers enjoy social interaction and teaching your dog tricks is a great way to spend some quality

*Here a Golden has learnt to catch a ball mid-air.*

time with him; it also teaches him to listen to you, burns excess energy and helps to relieve stress. Golden Retrievers are highly intelligent dogs and enjoy stretching their mind to learn new things, which also beats boredom. Tricks can actually be used to teach and reinforce commands; they can even be incorporated as a fun element into everyday commands that the Golden can sometimes 'play deaf to'. Even tricks unrelated to commands are a great way to spice up training as they are fun and there's no pressure to do it 'correctly'.

Young puppies and elderly dogs should not be expected to perform physically or mentally demanding tricks such as jumping or crawling along the floor; the strain on their body can affect joints or cause back problems.

When you are teaching your dog new tricks remember that training should be fun for your dog and easy for him to understand, so be clear with your signals – new tricks need body language and a verbal cue. Don't force your dog to perform a trick that he doesn't want to do; it may be that it causes him discomfort. Be careful with your tone of voice; keep training fun and light-hearted. If your dog isn't catching on as quickly as you would like, don't get angry with him; instead try it again later or another day. Only ask once: this rule applies as much to tricks as it does to commands; talking to your dog not only confuses him, but will teach him to ignore you.

Remember that Golden Retrievers are big dogs and so physically cannot do some tricks that smaller dogs can master easily. Below is a list of some basic tricks that are suitable for Goldens.

### Paw

First, ask your dog to sit. Next, lightly touch behind your dog's elbow, which will encourage him to lift that leg. Paw is taught by then taking up the dog's foot very gently, rewarding with praise and a treat the moment the paw is lifted up and in your hand. Once you have picked the foot up several times, try just holding your hand out, palm side up; when the paw is given freely, praise and reward and say 'paw'. Your Golden will soon learn this easy trick and be offering you his paw whenever there is food about or when he wants your attention.

*This Golden has learnt how to balance a treat on the end of his nose.*

You can also teach him to give paw and other paw. In the same way you can teach your dog to give you one paw and then the other on command by teaching paw for both front legs.

### Spin

This is a fun and easy trick to teach. With your dog standing up, hold a treat by his nose and then move it back towards his rear end; as he follows the treat, he will move his body around and be facing away from you. Bring the treat full circle back to where his nose originally was. Reward when a full circle is completed. Goldens are big dogs and you will need to give him room to move himself around in a circle.

Once your dog has got the hang of following the treat, incorporate the command 'spin' and bring the treat higher up from your dog, but making the same circle. Always ask your dog to complete a full circle before giving a treat, so he has to figure out what he needs to do to get the reward. Once he gets the idea you can pick up the speed.

### Roll over

Rolling over is fairly straightforward to teach if your Golden knows the 'lie down' command sufficiently. First, ask your dog to lie down. Once on the ground, take a biscuit from his nose and down along his body towards the rear end, keeping the treat as close to the body as you can. As your dog follows the treat, he will 'fold' himself and at this point you should take the treat over his body, like a rainbow, towards the ground on the other side. This will encourage your dog to roll onto his back and flip over to the other side. Reward him when he has completed his roll all the way over. It make take some dogs several attempts before they understand what is being asked of them, so just keep trying until they get the hang of it.

### Bow

This is a harder trick to do but good fun for the enthusiastic Golden. With your dog standing up, take a treat and place it between his front feet, pushing towards his back feet. As your dog moves his head down and crouches, reward him. Rewarding all the small movements will prevent him from going into a 'lie down' position. Incorporate the word 'bow' so your dog knows it is a new command, and keep taking the treat further back towards his hind legs to see if he can bow all the way to the floor and hold the position. It may take a few attempts to master this trick but it is a great alternative to the usual tricks.

Remember: don't be mean with treats. The reward of food keeps a Golden enthusiastic and will make learning something new really worthwhile. At the end of training play with your dog; it ends the training on a good note and your Golden will enjoy some down-time after training.

## OVER-EXCITEMENT

If your dog becomes over-excited when you come home or someone enters the house, ignore him and tell other people to ignore him when they enter the house. If he jumps up, calmly walk away or go into another room. Do not say anything, and do not make eye contact with him. When your dog settles, go and praise him or give him a treat and allow the visitor to praise him. If he gets excited again, go back to ignoring him. Your dog will soon learn that only good, calm behaviour gets noticed and rewarded.

If your dog gets over-excited without apparent reason (perhaps running around erratically or doing laps around the house or garden), it may be he has excess energy to burn off. He needs to release energy every day, and the amount of exercise he needs will depend on his energy levels. If your dog has been exercised but is still full of energy, you may need to increase the time he is walked or played with. Encourage games that incorporate mental stimulation, such as hiding toys, getting him to retrieve objects or teaching tricks. Mental stimulation can actually provide a better release of energy than physical exercise.

Some dogs become over-excited when they see another dog. You should allow your dog to play with other dogs to release energy and interact. Not allowing your dog to play with other dogs will only increase his frustration. Ensure that play sessions take place in a

*Always end training with a game or allow your dog some play time to keep things interesting.*

secure area, and the other dog's owner is happy to let them play.

Bear in mind that your dog may not be able to play with every dog he meets, so it is important to be able to keep your dog under control. Place him in a sit position and encourage him to watch you as the other dog comes closer; this can be done with treats or a favourite toy. When the other dog passes by, reward your dog for focusing on you. If your dog shows no interest in you at all, increase the distance between your dog and the other dog. This method of focus training also works if your dog gets over-excited when meeting people. Encourage other people not to interact with your dog and to simply walk by; your dog will learn that

**Top Tip**

Many dogs will happily do a trick as it nearly always ends with a reward, whereas many commands are given without a treat and the dog is simply expected to obey. Keep rewarding your dog every time he carries out a command, even if it is just praising with your voice, a stroke or a treat for every other command, and you will get good results every time you ask.

*Ensure your dog is in a secure environment if he is prone to running off after other things of interest.*

you are the most interesting person and that rewards come from you.

One of the most important things to remember is to always try to remain calm. Do not lose your temper, get frustrated, or become angry, or your dog will pick up on that negative energy and become even more excitable. If you find yourself getting frustrated, walk away and calm down; by the time you go back to your dog he will probably have calmed down too.

Remember that training is about practice, patience and persistence. If your dog will not carry out a command for you, and gets over-excited, walk away and let him calm down. Only when you and your dog are both calm should you try again, taking each command slowly and calmly.

## BOREDOM BUSTERS

Golden Retrievers are intelligent dogs and without sufficient stimulation they can get bored. Puppies tend to receive a lot of interaction as they require a lot of your attention and you are training them, but as a dog gets older sometimes our interaction with them lessens. Soon we get into a routine and forget that our dogs rely solely on us to keep them mentally as well as physically challenged. Taking your dog out for their daily walk may not cut it for some Goldens, and boredom may creep in. This can lead to destructive behaviour, such as stealing items, digging or even chewing.

To keep your dog's mind healthy and happy, try some of the following boredom busters.

### Tennis treats

Equipment needed: a muffin tin or cupcake tray (with four or six holes will be enough), treats and tennis balls (the same number as there are muffin/cake holes).

Take the tray and place a treat in the bottom of each hole. Next balance a tennis ball on each hole so it covers the treat. Put the tray on the floor and encourage your dog to sniff around the tray so he is interested. Lift one tennis ball to show him the treat and then put it back. Your Golden may initially use his nose to push the tennis balls out of the way, but if they are a snug fit, he will soon learn it is easier to pick the balls out to get to the treats. Once your dog has mastered how to get the treats out, this will soon become a favourite game and is a great way to distract your dog.

### Find the treat

Equipment needed: a large treat and a towel (you could use a clean dog towel).

Lay the towel out flat and place the treat in the centre of it (the treat needs to be quite large so it can be found easily). Wrap the towel around the treat and scrunch it into a ball. Then give the scrunched-up towel to your dog and let him figure out how to get to the treat. Most

*Goldens enjoy a good dig!*

Goldens will dig at the towel, while some will take their time and unwrap it with their teeth. The first time you show this to your dog, make sure it is easy for him to get to the treat or he will become frustrated. Once he knows there is a treat inside, he will put in extra effort to find it the next time.

### Pick the pot

Equipment needed: three plastic flower pots and one treat.

Turning the flower pots upside down, place the treat under one of them, showing your dog what you are doing. Move the flower pots around on the ground so you do not give away which one holds the treat. Now let your dog figure out which flower pot has the treat underneath. He will likely use his nose to push over small flower pots, but if you use a slightly larger size he will be inclined to use his feet, providing more stimulation and making the game harder.

*Find the treat in a towel.*

# CHAPTER 9

# CARING FOR YOUR DOG

## EXERCISE

Golden Retrievers were bred to work for a living, to earn their keep. The most common job for them today is as companions, which, coupled with our busy lifestyles, can lead to a mostly confined, isolated and inactive life. Golden Retrievers require physical and mental stimulation to relieve their natural working tendencies, and a lack of purpose can result in behavioural problems such as excessive barking, digging, stealing, chewing, destructive behaviour and hyperactivity.

Your dog needs the opportunity to exercise every day. Exercise is a vital ingredient in having a happy, healthy and well-rounded dog. Exercise:

- gives your dog a chance to relieve himself;
- allows for socialization with other animals and people;
- burns off excess energy, helping to eliminate behaviour issues such as digging, chewing, and hyperactivity;
- helps to reduce digestive problems;

*Two Goldens tired after a long walk.*

- builds your dog's confidence in unfamiliar places; and
- helps keep his weight under control.

Do not assume that letting your dog out in the garden will give him the exercise he needs, as most Goldens, after relieving themselves and having a play with a toy, will lie down again, preferably in the sun.

The most obvious form of exercise is to go for a walk. This should begin during puppyhood. It is very tempting, however, to over-exercise young puppies because they are so full of energy, but too much exercise when young can lead to health problems such as hip dysplasia in later life.

Very long or energetic dog walks, such as running alongside you on a bike, are best saved until your puppy is over a year old, as are strenuous activities such as agility. Try not to let your puppy play very rough games with much bigger dogs as his muscles and tendons will still be soft at a young age. Boundless puppy energy can be released through play and training.

As a rough guide, puppies can be allowed ten to fifteen minutes of walking at three to four months old, twenty minutes at four to six months, thirty to forty minutes at six to ten months and at one year old they should be having at least forty-five minutes of exercise, which can be split throughout the day.

Fully grown Goldens are generally happy with as little or as much exercise as you want to give them. However, although they will seem quite content to spend all day sleeping in front of the fire, your dog should be walked every day for at least an hour, and if you can spare the time for two hours. If you have a dog from working bloodlines, you will find his natural tendency to work is greater than in show-type dogs and he will require more exercise and interaction.

Walking should be a chance not just for exercise, but to spend quality time with your dog; most importantly, it should be fun. Doing the same walk day-in and day-out can be dull. Try to vary your walks so you are not doing the same route every day. Play games with your dog: don't just take a ball to play fetch, try hiding behind a tree when your dog isn't watching and then calling him to you.

Try other activities such as agility. If you don't have

*Swimming can be incorporated into a walk and Goldens have a natural love for water.*

an agility group nearby, try putting up some jumps in your garden with some garden canes and upturned buckets. Dogs love games of chase, so why not play like a dog: chase your dog and then run away, encouraging him to come after you, and then swap and chase your dog again. Golden Retrievers won't need much encouragement to take part in this game.

Try to go somewhere new every month, like visiting a wood or a beach. Or try swimming. Goldens are naturals when it comes to water and swimming, and they do not need to be asked even once about going in. There are dog pools available for swimming, but a clean, safe river or beach will do. Do not let your dog swim too far out, though, or in choppy waters in case he should get into trouble and you will need to go and get him.

Remember: dogs need exercise every day, come rain or shine.

## PLAYTIME

Play is vital for dogs; it is their main source of pleasure. By involving yourself in your dog's games, you too will become a source of pleasure for your dog. Playing with your Golden Retriever will provide him with the chance to display what comes naturally to him. Especially if he does not work, your Golden will enjoy the physical and mental similarities between playing and working.

Playing games is not just for puppies; it develops a bond between you and your dog. Playtime is fun for your dog and it also channels his energy and is a good source of exercise. But what many people don't know is that playing is more than that. It establishes trust, friendship and respect. If you play regularly with your dog, no matter his age, you will become the most interesting person in the world to him. When you are the centre of your Golden's world, he is less likely to look for other dogs to play with or run off to entertain himself.

Games provide physical and mental stimulation, and Golden Retrievers, as working dogs originally, will thrive on having something to do. Having an outlet in playtime will also reduce any boredom games that Goldens often love, such as stealing items like shoes that will encourage you to chase them.

There are lots of games to play; some include toys and others not. You do not have to spend a fortune to

*Children and Goldens make excellent play friends as children enjoy their funny antics.*

*Goldens love a soft cuddly toy which they can carry around.*

play with your Golden; most enjoy retrieving a bundle of old socks just as much as a new plush toy.

Goldens like soft cuddly toys that they can mouth and carry around easily. This type of toy is perfect for retrieving games inside the house or as a comforter. Balls are another favourite toy as they are fun to chase, as are Frisbees or other long-distance games, and they are perfect toys to take with you on a walk. Tug-of-war games with a rope will provide some variety, as will rubber and squeaky toys.

Like children, dogs do get bored of the same toy, so having a range of toys (and removing them after playtime) will keep things interesting for your Golden.

Toys can be much more than an item that gets picked up every now and then. Goldens love bringing a toy to a friend and some are known to empty their toybox in the pursuit of showing off all their toys to a new arrival in the house. Goldens are not generally destroyers of toys, and instead prefer to carry them around, their toys can last many years and many Goldens will have their favourites.

Everyone can get involved with playtime; by involving the whole family your dog is building a relationship with everyone and becomes, quite literally, part of the family. Bring toys with you when out on a walk and allow each member of the family to take it in turns to throw the toy. If you haven't taken a toy out with you on a walk, you can still play games with your dog as a family; take it in turns to hide somewhere and encourage your dog to go and find each person. Children are often better at playing games than adults as they have no inhibitions and will quite happily run around, roll on the floor and laugh. Goldens love silly games, so be as silly as you like!

Puppies need to be played with more frequently throughout the day, but adult dogs will enjoy playing with you at least once every day. Playing doesn't need to last for very long and you can have a few games throughout the day. Next time you come home and your Golden brings you a toy, spend a few minutes playing with him. He will be overjoyed that you accepted his invitation to play and the result is a happy dog.

## TYPES OF GAME

### Retrieve

Retrieving games do not always have to consist of throwing a toy out and your Golden fetching it back to you. Make it more interesting by hiding a toy and sending your dog to find it. With a young Golden make it easy to start with; hide a toy in the same room and somewhere relatively easy to find, like behind the sofa. As your dog becomes more adept at using his senses to locate the toy, make it more difficult by hiding it in another room, under a blanket or out in the garden. Always make a huge fuss of your dog when he returns with the toy and reward him when he drops it.

### Tug-of-war

The tug-of-war game is loved by all dogs at all ages; they will happily pull the toy while you gently pull back. Use a toy that is long enough so your hand is not too close to your dog's mouth, such as a rope toy. This game can become very exciting, so incorporating some commands, such as the 'leave it' command, into it will stop things from getting out of hand. When you play tug-of-war with your Golden, make sure you win more than you lose. Do not win all the time as your dog will become bored of the game, but if you let him win all the time, he will think he is stronger than you. By winning three out of five games you are giving your dog the right message and still enjoying a good game.

### Chase

Chase games involve toys such as tennis balls or Frisbees. As with the retrieve, you are throwing out a toy for your dog to chase after and bring back to you. The difference is in the distance and speed. Chase games are best done outside in an open space such as a field where you can really throw the toy and your dog will exert himself in chasing it. Frisbees and tennis balls on a throwing stick can go some distance; start small to begin with so your dog has a chance to chase after it without it going out of sight. You can make this game harder for your dog by asking him to wait while you throw it and then sending him off to find it. Your Golden will enjoy searching for his toy as it brings out his natural behaviour and keeps the game interesting.

### Hide and seek

This game, when played during a walk, is a great way to teach your dog to watch you. You can duck behind trees when he's not looking and then call him to find you. Your Golden will relish having to use his senses to find you and he will enjoy the hunt. Make sure, though, that you can keep an eye on your dog when playing this game to ensure he doesn't go off in completely the wrong direction and become panicked because he can't find you. This game doesn't just have to be played outside; you can play hide and seek in your house too. Leaving your dog in one room, go and hide in another room and then ask him to come and find you. You can be as imaginative as you like, and hide behind sofas, the curtains or even in a wardrobe. Once your dog gets the idea, you can make it more difficult too and play hide and seek elsewhere.

### Catch

This game is a little more one-sided than the child's equivalent (tag) in that your dog is the one chasing after you all the time. Encouraging your dog to run after you as you run away is a great way of showing your dog that he has to keep up with you. It will teach him to pay more attention to where you are if you are unpredictable in this game. (By unpredictable, I mean you randomly run away from him without giving him notice that you are about to do so.)

To start, run in the opposite direction from your dog, calling him in an excited tone until he starts chasing after you. Once the chase begins, it's a matter of keeping running until he catches up. This game works perfectly out on a walk and can be done with several people, with everyone taking it in turns to run away. As Goldens love a game of chase, you won't have to put in much encouragement to get him to chase after you; he will love racing around between people and getting lots of fuss when he 'catches' someone.

There are so many games that you can play with your dog, all of which will keep you both active and build on the relationship you share. Playing should be fun for both you and your Golden, so don't worry if your dog isn't playing by the rules or doesn't understand what it is you're asking him to do; just enjoy it! It is so easy to rush a walk because you don't have enough time, or to go for days without playing with your dog because you're too busy. Playing doesn't need to take up much time and you should be able to incorporate a little play every day, even if it is just for a few minutes.

## FEEDING

Knowing what, when and how much to feed your puppy or dog can be a minefield.

Puppies should be on four meals a day; they develop very quickly and need suitable nourishment. They require more protein than adult dogs and some dog foods specialize in puppy food with a higher protein level. Wherever you buy your puppy from, find out what food he is used to. It is best to keep your puppy on the same food initially; when the time comes to change the food, or you would like to change your puppy's diet, it needs to be done gradually over a matter of weeks so as not to upset his stomach.

Do not be alarmed if your new puppy goes off his food for a few days here and there; it is quite normal. The best plan of action is to stick with the food your puppy is used to, as new experiences and excitement can often put puppies off; your puppy may also be having a higher number of treats than normal in his training sessions. If your puppy goes off his food for more than a few days, or looks under the weather and is starting to lose weight, seek advice from your vet, as there may be a health problem. If you have a puppy (or even a dog) who goes through phases of leaving food,

*Two Goldens waiting eagerly for their dinner.*

do not be tempted to keep changing their diet as this will only encourage fussy eating.

If your puppy or dog is particularly fussy and is losing weight (but there is not an underlying health issue), then it often helps to add a little meat, fish or scrambled egg. Alternatively, try soaking the biscuits in warm water or adding a little goat's milk (not cow's milk as it is not as easy to digest). If your dog is not losing weight and is just being fussy on occasions, do not pander to him; no dog will starve himself.

If your puppy or dog has loose stools, try adding a little natural yoghurt to their biscuit, or plain chicken and rice to ease any upset stomach.

If your dog walks away from the food you put down, pick it up. Do not leave food down for your dog; instead, put it back down for their next meal. If you leave it down it will not only attract flies in warmer weather but also produce picky eaters who will happily graze during the day or hold out until you offer them a tastier meal (such as scraps). Dogs will get hungry eventually and when they realize that a different meal will not be offered, they will eat their food.

It is important that you are able to handle your puppy or dog safely should you need to take food away from him in instances where the item he is eating is inedible or it is not acceptable to eat or chew.

Some puppies/dogs become food aggressive, which is not surprising as they will be used to competing for food. To stop this, while your puppy or dog is eating, offer him something yummier to eat. He will leave his dinner and take the treat you have offered. It is important that you do not take his dinner bowl away, and you must allow him to go back to eating once he has had the treat. Once that is successful, you can start adding extra food into the dinner bowl (again without lifting it away), so you are adding more treats to his dinner. Your dog will soon learn that your hand being near his food does not mean you will take the food away but provide more treats.

Once your dog is fine with you adding food to his bowl, you can lift the bowl up and add a little extra food to it before putting it back down again, so it becomes a good experience for him when the bowl is lifted up. If your dog is happy with you doing this, do not keep taking food away as this too can cause territorial behav-

iour, which is why swapping food for something better and then putting the dinner back is a kinder option and your dog will not feel threatened. If your dog is not food or toy possessive, leave him to eat in peace; only if there are signs of territorial behaviour should these exercises be repeated.

Goldens, like all dogs, need a balanced diet of carbohydrates, protein, fats, vitamins and minerals. Dog kibble provides all of this and is convenient, mess free and easily stored. There is an ever-increasing variety of dog food available to suit everyone's needs and budgets. Options include:

- biscuit kibble
- tinned
- frozen
- sachet
- raw/natural.

If you have a working Golden Retriever you will need a type of dog food specifically formulated for working dogs to sustain the stamina needed for working all day in the field.

The raw diet is increasing in popularity as owners become more aware and concerned about what is in processed dog food such as tinned meat, kibble and sachet food. Mimicking the natural diet of dogs in the wild, the idea is to provide unprocessed, raw food (including meat). It is completely natural and

*A combination of dog biscuit mixed with raw meat.*

dogs can consume all parts of an animal, including the organs and bones. It is only when they are cooked that bones become brittle and therefore dangerous when consumed. Feeding the raw diet improves digestion, produces firmer stools, reduces allergy symptoms, simplifies weight management and results in a healthy coat. Should you choose to select and prepare the food yourself, ensure you are providing your dog with the balanced needs essential for good health. Something to bear in mind, and potentially a very serious matter, is the presence of bacteria; salmonella and E. coli germs are a potential and severe risk in raw meats. If the meat you have purchased smells bad or is discoloured, do not feed it to your dog.

Alternatively, there are a number of raw food suppliers where the meat is mixed with vegetables and grains and includes all the other nutritional elements your dog needs; it is frozen for convenience but should always be defrosted before being given to your dog. This is the most popular form of feeding the raw diet, along with mixing raw meats with kibble.

It is best to seek detailed advice from your vet, a dog nutritionist or a reliable local pet store about the types of food available; they will be able to advise you on the nutritional values of the different types and suggest the most suitable for your dog.

### Top Tip

Remember to always have fresh water available for your dog. Your dog's water bowl should be emptied every day and fresh water put down. During the summer months you may need to top it up a couple of times during the day. It is not acceptable to remove water when you leave your dog or limit the amount of water your dog drinks to stop him from toileting.

Throughout the life of your dog you may need to change his diet to suit his needs. As your dog increases in age, his nutritional requirements change; adolescents with high energy levels may benefit from a low-protein mix to reduce their energy levels, while older dogs will need a senior mix that often include supplements for joint problems.

## OBESITY

Obesity in any dog is a serious matter. Golden Retrievers love their food and great care must be taken to ensure they do not gain excess weight. Obesity puts strain on the joints and heart; Goldens are prone to hip dysplasia, which, although mostly a hereditary disease,

*You should weigh your Golden every time you go to the vet.*

can also be caused by obesity. It is vital that your dog's weight is monitored for a healthy and ultimately happy life.

- Keep a record of your dog's weight every time you visit the vet.
- Monitor how many treats are being given on a daily basis.
- Do not give your dog scraps from your dinner regularly.
- Do not feed your dog fatty or sugary foods.
- Reduce his food quantity on days where exercise is limited.

Puppies need to grow and develop, but it is important for future health that a puppy grows in a controlled and gradual way. The mistake many owners make with a young puppy is actually underfeeding, especially if they have a greedy puppy. Puppies do require more calories, proteins, minerals and vitamins than adult dogs, but as they develop and grow this need lessens. Puppy food has higher levels of protein and calories, which can produce unruly behaviour in an adolescent. Your puppy should have changed from puppy food to adult food by the time he is one year old.

It can be quite difficult to see if a puppy is the correct weight, not least because Golden puppies have a lot of excess skin. As a rough guide, puppies should be shapely with a little round tummy and some excess skin. If the tummy is quite large and firm, and there is only a little excess skin, they are having too much food.

Too much food combined with too little exercise is the main ingredient for obesity. During the summer months people tend to live more active lifestyles, and during the winter tend to be more homebound. It often becomes the routine to give your dog the same amount of food every day, but his weight can creep up in the winter period if exercise is limited. Your dog's food quantity needs to be adjusted accordingly during these months.

For the correct amount to feed your dog, base the quantity on how your dog looks and feels, rather than following packet guidelines. Even dogs of the same size and weight can have different quantity requirements. If your dog has a very energetic lifestyle and you do activities such as running with him, he will require more food for energy than a dog of the same weight who does an hour's walk every day.

Neutering can have an effect on your dog's weight as it slows down the metabolic rate, especially in bitches. If you do neuter your dog, feeding will need to be reduced slightly.

When reducing food, do it gradually over a period of days. Your dog will be used to larger quantities and will end up hungry if the amount is reduced too quickly, which could lead to stealing food. For the best results, decrease food gradually and increase exercise gradually. This will lead to a dog who gains fitness in a controlled manner, and so is therefore more likely to maintain the ideal weight.

---

**Top Tip**

As a guide to see if your adult dog is the correct size, you should be able to feel but not see his ribs. Run your hands down his body; he should curve inwards at the waist. If you cannot feel the ribs and there is no curve at the waist, your dog is probably overweight. If you are uncertain whether your dog is the correct weight, ask your vet for advice.

---

## DAILY CHECKS

Daily checks are useful for when the vet needs to check over your dog and if your dog is looked after by another person. He will be more willing to be handled by others if he is used to it.

Daily checks should include running your hands all over his body. Goldens have long hair that can hide all sorts, so it is important that you check to make sure there are no foreign bodies sticking in the skin or tangled in the hair; it also gets your dog used to being stroked all over his body.

Run your hands down all four legs and carefully lift each paw, feeling in between the toes. Do not bend your dog's legs at an angle to see the pads, but flex the joint to check the pads.

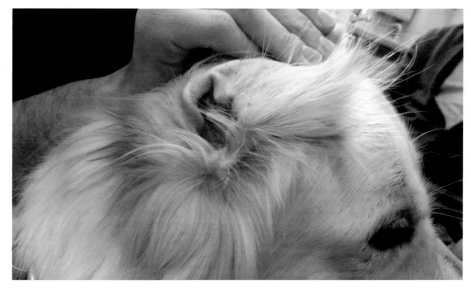

*Lift your dog's ear up and over the head to check it is clean and without inflammation or soreness.*

Next, gently lift each ear, making sure it is clean and sweet-smelling; any foul smell or patchy hair can be an indication of an ear infection or mites.

To check the mouth, gently open the jaws by using your thumb. Do not try to force your dog to open his mouth, or you may get bitten by accident. To start with, just open the mouth for a few seconds and release. Build up the time until you can easily inspect the teeth and gums. The gums should be pink and smooth. Any sign of infection or disease will leave the gums inflamed, red, sore and possibly bleeding.

To clean his teeth you must use toothpaste specifically formulated for dogs, which is flavoured, protects their teeth and combats the problems associated with canine teeth. It also does not froth. Never be tempted to use on your dog toothpaste intended for human use.

Check his eyes are not runny or gunky; they should be clear and bright. There is no need to lift the eyelids as you should just be able to see the whites of the eyes to make sure they are not bloodshot.

Finally, check under the tail for faeces. As the coat is thick, this area needs to be kept clean, especially when your dog gets older and loses the flexibility to clean that area.

## TRAVELLING

Your dog will undoubtedly make quite a few car jour-neys during his life and it is important that he gets used to car journeys and that your car is suitable for him.

From a young age (ideally as soon as you get your dog), take short car journeys with him on at least a weekly basis. This will ensure he gets used to going into a car without much fuss and travel sickness will ease in time. Before heading off on any journey, ensure your dog has been to the toilet and don't go out just after he has eaten a meal, as it may come back up again on the journey.

A young puppy can be placed on a passenger's lap for the first few outings, but make sure he does not pose a distraction to the driver or the results could be fatal. As Goldens are large dogs, they should ideally be placed in the back of the car. Your car should be large enough for your dog to stand up fully and turn around with ease; large hatch-backs, estate cars, 4X4s or vans are most suitable. Dogs should never be placed in the boot of a saloon car.

Invest in a crate that fits into your car; this will give him a secure place which can contain his bed, toys and water bowls, as well as give him some protection should you be involved in a car accident. At the minimum insert a barrier between the boot and the seats; this will prevent your dog being thrown forward over the seats in the event of a collision.

If you decide to place your dog on the back seat of your car, he should wear a specially designed harness

*Ensure your vehicle is suitable for your dog/s when travelling.*

that allows the seatbelt to be secured around him, again for safety. It also stops the dog from moving around too much and potentially becoming a distraction for the driver.

**Top Tip**

If your dog barks in the car at passers-by or other dogs, place a light sheet over his crate or use sun visors to block him from being able to look out of the windows. A dog barking, howling or jumping around when you are driving can be a huge distraction and very dangerous if you are paying more attention to him than to the road. It is far better to put him in a crate and place a blanket over it to help him relax.

## HANDLING AND GROOMING

Goldens have the most irresistibly soft, hand-inviting fur and will undoubtedly get lots of attention. Getting your dog used to being stroked and touched is beneficial as there will always be people, especially children, who will want to stroke him. Goldens are excellent at tolerating our needs, and will put up with being patted on the head and having arms thrown around their neck. But it important to remember that stroking is preferable, as it is calming, soothing and relaxing. It builds up trust that human hands are not a threat but a pleasurable experience.

When you lift up your puppy, make sure you do so carefully, so as not to cause any discomfort or anxiety if he feels insecure. For a secure hold, place one hand underneath both armpits and the other hand underneath his bottom, tucking the tail in. Your puppy will not stay small for long, so try not to let him get too used to being picked up or you may find you have a fully grown adult wanting to sit on your lap at any given opportunity. Handling should be enjoyable, but try to encourage calm behaviour as otherwise it can quickly turn into a game every time you want to handle your dog.

### Top Tip

If, during handling and grooming checks, you find your dog wants to play, use a chew treat or a toy to distract him and move your hands slowly to encourage him to relax. If your dog gets very wound up, let him go, and try to groom him later on. Goldens have a thick coat that moults all year long, so you will need to groom him at least once a week, and he will soon get used to the process if it is done regularly.

Practising gentle restraint is important as there will be some situations where it will be necessary, either for your dog's safety or to protect others. The first time most dogs experience restraint is at the vets, which is shortly followed by an injection or other unpleasant and painful experience.

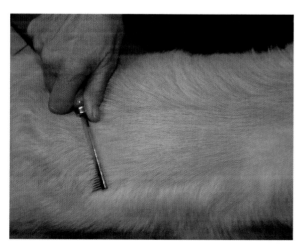

*Using a wide-tooth comb will untangle the Golden's thick coat.*

*A selection of grooming brushes and equipment.*

To get your dog used to gentle restraint, first place your hands on one side of the body and on the chest. (It may be worth tucking your dog's bottom between your legs so he is facing away from you; this will stop him trying to walk away.) Once he has relaxed under this gentle restraint, let him go and allow him to move around freely so it is a happy experience and not one that will make him fear the consequences every time he is restrained.

Grooming your Golden will be necessary to ensure your dog has a beautiful, mat-free coat (not to mention less of it on your floor). Grooming is also a good way to bond with your dog as most Goldens enjoy a good pampering. Bitches will moult more during their season and need to be brushed daily, otherwise a thorough brush every other day is sufficient. If your dog does not like being groomed, or wants to play with the brush, do not reprimand him, as it should be an enjoyable experience and you will certainly be doing a fair amount of it.

Begin by using a soft body brush and gently run it over the coat, following the flow of the hair. Use a suitable brush to groom the moulting coat; Goldens have a dense, waterproof undercoat and there are brushes available specifically for this undercoat. Again, run the brush over the coat in the direction of the hair, paying particular attention to the chest and hindquarters where there is an abundance of fur.

**Top Tip**

If the hair is very matted and cannot be brushed out, very carefully trim it away using scissors. Use a brush or your fingers to lift the matted hair away from the skin, ensuring you do not accidentally cut your dog. As Golden Retrievers have such a thick coat, it is important they are groomed regularly to avoid any matting.

A finer-toothed comb can be used to brush the fur on the ears, down the legs and the tail, taking great care not to pull the skin if the fur is knotted. Lastly, trim any excess fur between the toes, being very careful not to cut the pads. Walking on tarmac will naturally help to keep these hairs short.

## BATHING

It is important to bath your dog, but done too often it can remove the natural oils that keep a dog's skin and coat healthy. Once a month is more than enough for a Golden, but you may find during the winter you need to wash your dog more often as the long coat can absorb dirt and can smell very 'doggy' when wet.

If you are not precious about your bathroom, place your Golden in your bath or shower; alternatively, fill a couple of buckets with warm water and take your dog into the garden (not recommended in winter). Rinse him with warm water, so he is wet all over. Using a dog

*For a Golden who is less than impressed by baths, it's worth having some extra hands on standby.*

shampoo, lather the coat as you would wash your own hair (being careful not to get shampoo in the eyes or ears). Then rinse out all the shampoo with warm water, making sure there is no soap left (double check his armpits and around his rear end as these areas often get missed). Gently rub your dog down with a dry towel until he is thoroughly dry. At this stage, most dogs get very excited and try to wriggle free and run around your house, so dry slowly and gently.

## NAIL CLIPPING

A dog's toenails can be very sharp and grow quite long if not blunted or shortened. For some dogs, having their toenails clipped is quite stressful, so it is best to introduce nail clipping at the puppy stage. This can be done using an emery board, with nail scissors or clippers specially designed for dogs. If using scissors or clippers, be very careful not to remove too much of the nail and reach the quick, as this will hurt your dog and cause bleeding.

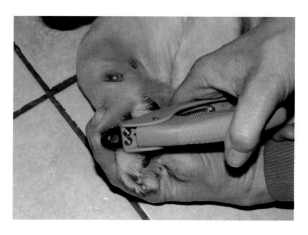

*Ensure your dog is calm and still before clipping his toe nails to ensure you do not take off too much.*

---

**Top Tip**

If your dog has clear-coloured nails, it is easier to see the quick, which will look like a pink diamond at the top of the nail. Most Goldens have black nails, making it far harder to see. As a guide, lift the foot up so you can see underneath the nails. The nail should be encased by the skin all the way around near the top and then hollow out near the end. It is the hollow part of the nail that can be trimmed. If you are uncertain, ask your vet to trim your dog's nails.

---

As a general rule, only the tip of the nail should be trimmed, where you can feel a curve in it. If you are in any doubt, ask your vet to show you what to do.

Walking on hard surfaces such as concrete pavements can keep nails shortened, saving you a job, but remember that too much road walking can cause problems such as hardening, scuffing and sore pads.

## THE OLDER DOG

Golden Retrievers have an average life expectancy of around twelve to fifteen years.

As your dog gets older his needs will change; he will slow down and appreciate the creature comforts and a quieter life. The routine you have both been used to for the majority of his life will need to be adapted into his senior years to ensure he is happy, healthy and comfortable.

It is important to have more regular check-ups at the vet. Your dog's health may deteriorate over time and your vet will be able to keep on top of any early signs of a serious illness. Any illnesses such as stomach upset and changed behaviour should receive medical attention, no matter how trivial; older dogs do not bounce back from problems as quickly as younger dogs and will need extra support for the immune system. It is possible that your dog will also require dentistry checks to ensure his teeth and gums are healthy and the build-up of plaque and tartar is kept to a minimum.

Your dog's coat will start to change as he ages. Most notable will be the whiter hairs on his face, especially around the muzzle. His coat will become thicker and potentially coarser. As his joints become stiffer, he will not be able to groom himself as much and so it is important to brush your dog regularly to keep his coat in good condition and prevent it from getting matted.

*Enjoying the simple pleasure of watching.*

### Top Tip

You can teach old dogs new tricks. No matter what his age is, keep his mind active and try new games and tricks. He will love the attention and enjoy reliving those puppy days of training. Just bear in mind that if he has stiff joints there may be some tricks he is unable to do, such as rolling over or jumping.

Your older dog should still have daily exercise, but at a pace that is suitable for him. Walks may have to be reduced in distance and pace if you notice he is struggling to keep up with you or if he needs to lie down and rest. Exercise should still be regular as it will help keep him young in mind and body. If you do take him out for long walks, remember to stop frequently so he can rest, and take plenty of water and some snacks for energy. Your dog should be towelled off after walks if he gets wet and muddy; older dogs will chill more easily if they are left to air dry.

As your dog ages his bladder will become weaker so he will need to be let out to relieve himself more frequently and, like a puppy, he should not be left alone for very long periods. His dietary needs will also change. You may find that smaller, more regular

*Still curious!*

meals are more suitable for your Golden. Be careful that his weight doesn't creep up; Golden oldies are prone to obesity in old age and their food will need to be changed to a senior mix.

You may find that your dog's sight and hearing may also fade and he will require a gentle approach to such changes. His bed should be kept in the same location and he will appreciate a more stable routine so he knows what to expect. Failing sight and hearing may mean your dog is more easily spooked. Pay attention to where your dog is walking so he doesn't bump into things, and try to avoid any sudden changes in light, such as turning on a bright light in a completely dark room.

Invest in a warm comfortable bed; your dog will spend more time in it and will need to be completely comfortable and warm. If he has stiff joints he will need support with mobility. As Goldens are large dogs, ramps can be useful for getting him in and out of vehi-

cles and up and down small stairs, rather than trying to lift him.

As old age comes, it is inevitable that your dog's health will start to deteriorate and you may be faced with the difficult decision of when to say goodbye. Nothing can quite prepare you for this time, but it is important to take into consideration his quality of life. If he is in pain or has a life-threatening illness that will cause him suffering, it is often kinder to relieve him of the pain and distress, and spare him his dignity. Your vet will guide you and support you in making the right decision, whether to let him go naturally or have him put to sleep.

Golden Retrievers have an expressive face, an apparent understanding, and when he is ready he will let you know. If you are keeping him alive because you cannot bear to part with him, remember that it is better to have the memory of your dog happy and with dignity, rather than watching him suffer that last stretch.

Of course, quality of life means different things to different people, but you know your dog better than anyone and will ultimately be able to make the right decision, whichever you should choose. When that dreaded time comes, you may decide you want to bury your beloved friend at home or have him cremated so you can spread his ashes in a special place.

The loss of a dog can be as great as losing a person you love, and unfortunately time is the only healer. Some people make the decision to get a new puppy quickly to ease the pain, whereas others cannot bear the thought of a replacement. Do take into account how others in the house may feel after the loss. This will not necessarily mean just human family members, but other pets too. For instance, has another dog been left alone and is pining for the company of their lost friend? Sometimes a new puppy can be a great distraction and giver of happiness for everyone.

Remember the good times that were shared and take comfort in knowing you will meet again at the rainbow bridge.

*A Golden is forever young at heart.*

# CHAPTER 10

# HEALTHIER DOGS ARE HAPPIER

## DAILY CHECKS

Taking care of your dog's health should not require a second thought; it is vital for a comfortable, happy and long life. Ill-health can come to any dog at any age, but there are steps that can be taken to ensure

your dog is healthy, and regular checks will mean that anything untoward can be found and treated immediately. Prevention is, after all, better than cure.

You, as the owner, can check on your dog's health every single day. It may be all too obvious if he is unwell, has hurt himself or behaves unusually when there is something seriously wrong, but carrying out daily checks brings you more in tune with your dog's health as you will know what is normal for him, and it can help in early diagnosis. Carry out your daily checks while grooming, paying close attention to his eyes, ears, feet, teeth and mouth, skin and coat, and genitals. Checking these areas closely will show if your dog is showing any signs of illness, leading to early diagnosis and treatment, potentially reducing any pain or significant illness.

## VET CHECK-UP

It is important to have a full health check and examination by your vet on an annual basis to ensure your dog is in good health. Dogs age at a far greater rate than humans do, and their health can change dramatically throughout the course of a year. Even monitoring your dog's weight every year has its uses as bodyweight can creep up without you noticing. The check-up can be done to coincide with the annual vaccination and will ensure there are no underlying problems and your dog is fit and healthy.

*The annual vet check is important to ensure your dog is fit and healthy.*

## ADMINISTERING MEDICATION

Worming tablets and other medication in tablet form is administered orally. You can pop the tablets in with food, although some dogs have the ability to eat the food and spit out the tablet, or will avoid eating the food at all. Dogs receiving medication should be monitored to ensure this does not happen.

Alternatively, open your dog's mouth and pop the tablet at the back of the mouth. Hold his mouth closed with one hand and with the other gently rub his throat, encouraging him to swallow. Liquids can be given in the same way (via a syringe).

## INSURANCE

Pet insurance can be very worthwhile; it provides peace of mind in case something happens without warning to your dog and he requires costly veterinary treatment. As medicines become more advanced, many new treatments are now available but they can be very expensive. Having insurance will allow your vet to select the best treatment for your dog, regardless of the cost. Some insurance companies also help with the costs of publicity if your dog goes missing and provide third party insurance to cover legal liability.

If your pet becomes unwell and is not already insured, you may find it difficult to obtain pet insurance. Many insurance companies will not cover a dog with a known illness, a particular condition or an illness from birth. If, however, you take out a policy when your pet is healthy, you will be covered for veterinary treatments and accidents, but remember always to check the small print before you take out a policy with any company.

The level of coverage in the policies varies, and will continue to do so as insurance companies compete with one another so it is often difficult to get an accurate recommendation. However, from experience, you should avoid the cheapest policies as they often limit the amount that can be claimed, have a higher excess, will not pay out for life-long illnesses, or will only cover costs for a period of time. As there are so many different options available, opt for a policy that suits you and your dog and preferably provides lifetime cover.

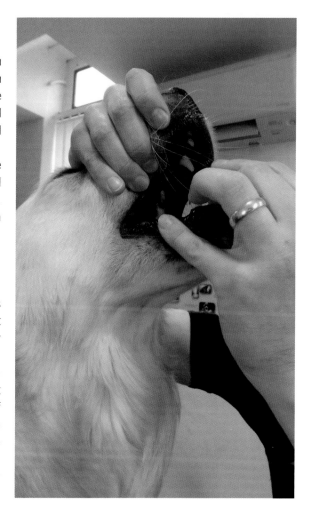

*Open your dog's mouth and pop the tablet towards the back of the throat.*

If you choose not to insure your dog, it is important to remember that the cost of treatment can run into hundreds and sometimes thousands, so make sure you are able to cover any costs that may arise. Owning a dog is a lifelong responsibility and we have a duty to ensure they are kept healthy and happy.

## MICROCHIPPING

Microchipping your dog provides a permanent and relatively inexpensive form of identification that cannot be lost or easily altered. It helps ensures that in the worst

*Insurance can provide peace of mind.*

case scenario of losing your dog, he can be reunited with your family.

Microchipping involves inserting a small microchip (about the size of a grain of rice) between the shoulder blades using a special needle. The implantation is similar to any other injection, except the needle is slightly larger.

Once the microchip is inserted, a scanner can be passed over the chipped area and the chip responds by transmitting its unique code to the scanner. Once this unique code is displayed on the scanner, the operator can refer to the national database to find your name, address and phone number.

It is recommended that you choose a veterinary

**Top Tip**

The chip itself does not hold your details, so it is vital that your details are updated on the national database (or with the company where your dog's microchip is registered) should you change your phone number, name or address. Your vet will be able to inform you which company your dog's microchip is registered with.

Microchips can also migrate around a dog's body, so it is worth having it scanned once a year by your vet to ensure it can still be found. If your dog's microchip does migrate, and is found, for example, when scanning the chest or a limb, add a note to that effect to your dog's tag.

surgery that uses microchips that are compatible with the European 'ISO' standard scanner. This means that the microchip can be read by scanners used by vets, inspectors, dog wardens and custom officials throughout Europe.

## DENTAL CARE

We brush our teeth every day to make sure they are clean and plaque is removed. But we often forget that our dogs' teeth also need to be brushed. Dental problems are among the most common health issues and yet one of the easiest to prevent. Getting your dog used to having his teeth brushed takes patience and persistence. Start by placing your fingers in and around your dog's mouth, and once he is happy to have your fingers running along his teeth, you can then progress to a finger brush or small toothbrush. To be shown how to brush your dog's teeth correctly and safely, speak to your veterinary nurse, who will be able to advise you.

Like us, dogs need toothpaste to clean their teeth. Remember, though, that human toothpaste is not suitable for dogs. Pet toothpaste has an enzymatic action on the plaque and tartar and is flavoured to your dog's taste (normally beef or poultry). Daily brushing will help reduce the build-up of tartar and plaque on your dog's teeth and reduce the need for ultrasonic scaling and polishing, which is carried out under anaesthetic by the vet to clean the teeth if there is a large build-up of both. If brushing your dog's teeth is impossible, there are other ways to help keep your dog's teeth healthy, such as providing a daily treat formulated to help reduce plaque and tartar, but these are less effective.

Dogs, like humans, have two sets of teeth. Puppy teeth normally start falling out around twenty weeks of age, and by around six months puppies will have the majority of their permanent adult teeth. When your puppy is teething, his gums may be very sore; providing toys designed for teething puppies will help to ease any discomfort. During teething, only gentle brushing is advisable.

Your dog's diet will play a part in contributing to healthy teeth; raw diets and dry foods and biscuits are much better than wet foods at reducing dental prob-

*It is important you check and clean your dog's teeth regularly.*

lems. If your dog shows any of the following signs, book an appointment with your vet or nurse: bad breath, loss of appetite, bleeding or inflamed gums, pawing at the mouth, difficulty eating, loose or missing teeth or excessive drooling.

## FLEA CONTROL

If you find fleas on your dog, the chances are there are also fleas in your household. Fleas lay their eggs on their host, which subsequently drop off. The eggs then hatch into larvae, which feed on dead skin cells

*When applying flea drops, part the fur so you can expose the skin to the treatment.*

in carpets and furnishings. The larvae will form into pupae, which can lie dormant for months before hatching into a flea. The new flea will then climb to the top of the carpet fibres and wait for the next host that passes by.

Fleas feed on the blood of their host, which causes irritation to the skin and results in frequent scratching. Some dogs can become allergic to the flea bites and develop flea allergy dermatitis, which is an itchy condition that causes hair loss.

If your dog has fleas, various treatments can be purchased from your vet; these are normally administered either every four weeks or every three months in the form of a liquid applied to the back of the neck

or between the shoulders, or in a spray or tablet form. All these kill the adult flea. There are also sprays available that can be used around the household; these not only kill adult fleas but prevent eggs and larvae from developing into adult fleas.

## TICKS, MITES AND LICE

Ticks wait at the top of long grass and attach themselves to dogs as they brush past, piercing a hole through the skin to feed on the dog's blood. They are easily spotted due to their bulbous abdomen, but removal requires skill as their heads must not be left inside the dog. Tick tweezers are recommended for easy removal as they ensure the tick is removed in its entirety. The most important risk associated with ticks is Lyme disease, which they can transmit. Prevention of ticks can come in the form of a medicated collar or in a combination product that eliminates fleas, ticks and lice.

Ear mites are highly contagious and can infect both dogs and cats. Living on the surface of the skin in the outer ear canal, they cause itching and inflammation and can lead to a more severe ear infection if left untreated. An infection often gives off a strong odour and a dark discharge in the ear. Treatments for ear mites include products applied directly to the ear, anti-inflammatory drugs and/or antibiotics. Ask your vet to be sure you administer the correct treatment for your dog, as the medication prescribed to treat ear mites is dependent on the severity of the infection. Regular

### Top Tip

Always ask your vet to recommend a product that is suitable for you and your dog. There are numerous products available which can be administered in different ways, and some tackle certain worms too. The cost of flea treatment can vary also and there is a temptation to purchase products off the shelf from pet stores, rather than through your vet. If you do decide to buy flea treatment from a store, ensure you read the packet carefully and administer the correct amount for your dog.

cleaning of the ear will assist in reducing an infection of ear mites.

Biting lice will spend their entire life-cycle on the host, with the transmission of lice occurring directly from contact with an infected dog; puppies and older dogs have a higher risk of being infected. Canine lice are not transferrable to humans or cats and are the easiest parasite to treat. Biting lice are very slow and share a resemblance with the head lice that infect humans, so are relatively easy to spot in your dog's coat. Severe infestations will cause intense itching, and damage to the skin from scratching is likely to result in inflammation, hair loss and infection. Treatment for lice is the same as for fleas, with many products containing combination treatments for fleas, ticks and lice.

*Your local county or district council supplies suitable bins for the disposal of dog waste; some also supply waste bags, as seen here.*

## WORMING

Most dogs do not show obvious signs of having worms; only if a dog is heavily infested will the intestines become blocked, causing weight loss, vomiting, bloat, diarrhoea and/or blood in the faeces. Dogs with tapeworms can have very small eggs in their faeces, which look similar to a grain of rice; their presence is among the easiest ways to tell if your dog has worms.

The most common types of worm that dogs pick up are roundworms, tapeworms, whipworms and hookworms, which live in the intestine.

Roundworms can be picked up by the dog eating the faeces of an infected animal, by eating a host (mouse or rat), or, in the case of puppies, through the placenta or milk from the mother. Nearly all puppies are born with worms due to dormant larvae in the bitch's body tissue that migrate to the placenta and mammary glands during pregnancy.

Tapeworms are often transmitted via fleas. Flea larvae eat the tapeworm eggs found in faeces. The flea larvae will then develop into an adult flea with the tapeworm egg lying dormant. When the dog licks himself for grooming, the flea is consumed, by default infecting the dog with tapeworm.

Humans can be infected with both roundworm and tapeworm, with the roundworm Toxocara Canis being particularly dangerous as it migrates within the tissues and can cause blindness if it moves to the back of the eye. Always pick up your dog's faeces and dispose of them responsibly to reduce environmental contamination.

Hookworms and whipworms feed on the blood from the intestinal lining and wall. Whipworms can be found in the large intestine, and the hookworms in the small intestine. Dogs are infected with whipworms and hookworms by ingesting the eggs or larvae. Hookworm larvae can also penetrate the skin, usually around the feet, causing infection.

Heartworms pose a threat to dogs throughout the world. Although they are not commonly found in the UK or Ireland, more cases are being reported as dogs contract them after travelling abroad without having suitable preventative treatment. Heartworms are transmitted by infected mosquitoes and, as their name suggests, live in the pulmonary arteries in the right side of the heart. Infection can be treated, but prevention is better than cure as an infection can develop into a life-threatening condition, causing high blood pressure, lethargy, heart failure and even death. If you are holidaying abroad, preventative treatment for heartworms should be started for your dog before you leave the UK and maintained during the visit.

Lungworms are less common, but can also be life-threatening as adult worms are found in the heart and pulmonary arteries and their eggs pass through the airways of the lungs. Dogs can become infected by consuming infected slugs, snails and frogs. Even if your dog does not actively eat slugs or snails, they can be swallowed by accident if your dog drinks from water outside (including puddles), picks up toys that have been left outside or is partial to eating sticks or grass. Symptoms vary but can include coughing, lethargy, weight loss, nose bleeds, bleeding in the eye, anaemia and excessive bleeding from minor wounds, with more severe symptoms including seizures, vomiting, diarrhoea, spinal pain and loss of appetite. If treated early, dogs can make a full recovery, so if you suspect that your dog has become infected with lungworm, seek veterinary attention immediately.

Breeders should worm puppies at two to three weeks old and at five to six weeks old, and possibly again before puppies go to their new homes. Puppies should then be wormed every three weeks until they are three months old, and then, like adults, every three months.

Treatments for worms will kill only the worms present on the day the treatment is given and will not protect the dog from reinfection, which is why regular treatment is the only way to ensure your dog is worm-free.

**Top Tip**

Discuss with your vet a suitable worming treatment and programme for your dog. There are some worming treatments that are combined with flea treatments and do not have to be orally administered. If the most suitable worming treatment for your dog is in tablet form, you can wrap it in a piece of food and give it to your dog.

Some dogs will do everything possible not to eat a tablet, and some can eat the food and then spit out the tablet. The easiest way to administer a tablet is to open the dog's mouth and pop in the tablet towards the back of his throat, then hold his mouth closed and tilt his head up slightly as you rub his throat to encourage him to swallow.

## RINGWORM

Ringworm, despite its name, is not actually a worm but a fungal infection. It is highly contagious and can spread between different species, including humans. The most common symptom associated with ringworm is lesions found on the limbs, head and ears, resulting in circular, scaly, bald spots . In severe cases ringworm can spread across the entire body; however, some dogs may be carriers of the fungus but not display any symptoms at all.

Younger dogs are at greater risk of contracting ringworm, as are dogs with a weaker immune system. Transmission of ringworm can occur through bedding, carpets, clothes and other materials that can collect infected hair or scales. Ringworm can also quickly spread through kennels and other places where there are lots of dogs in close proximity.

The treatment of ringworm will depend on the severity of the condition. As well as oral medication, there are medicated shampoos and ointments, and dips such as lime sulphur, which will kill the fungus. In severe cases both forms of treatment may be used. It is vital that treatment is carried out for the whole of the recommended period, even if the lesions begin to heal, as the healing of the lesions does not necessarily mean the dog is cured or cannot transmit the infection. Diagnostic tests may need to be carried out after treatment to ensure the infection has cleared, but this does not provide a guarantee that re-infection will not occur.

As the fungus can live in the environment for several months on materials, it is important to follow your vet's instructions in order to ensure the ringworm is not spread to other animals or people in the household. To reduce the risk of transmission, wash other pets in the medicated shampoo, wash or discard any bedding that the dog sleeps on, wash or discard his equipment or toys, vacuum frequently and thoroughly wash your hands after you bathe or touch your dog.

## VACCINATION

All puppies and dogs should be vaccinated against parvovirus, leptospirosis, distemper virus, infectious hepatitis virus and parainfluenza. These viruses are

*Vaccination is done annually; your vet will be able to advise which vaccinations are due.*

common and can be very severe. A vaccine against kennel cough is also needed if your dog goes into boarding kennels, and it is also recommended if you attend dog shows or indeed go anywhere with a high concentration of dogs.

Parvovirus is highly resistant in the environment, and direct contact with an infected dog is not needed. Parvovirus causes severe vomiting and diarrhoea, and in susceptible puppies can result in death.

Leptospirosis is usually caught through contact with rodent urine (often present in stagnant water), or from urine from an infected dog. A sudden severe infection can cause fever, vomiting, dehydration and death, whereas a chronic infection can lead to progressive kidney and/or liver failure.

Distemper is usually caught when an infected dog coughs or sneezes and the 'aerosol' produced comes into contact with another dog. The distemper virus initially causes a fever and can lead to vomiting, diarrhoea, coughing, cracking of the nose, hardened foot pads, fits and, on occasion, pneumonia.

Infectious hepatitis is caught from contact with urine, faeces or saliva from an infected dog. Once infected with the disease there is often violent vomiting and a painful abdomen; the dog can collapse quickly from shock, which often leads to death. A 'blueness' of the eye may also be noticeable.

Kennel cough (*Bordetella Bronchiseptica*) is caught through direct contact with an infected dog, or by simply being near an infected dog when he coughs.

As the name implies, kennel cough causes coughing, occasionally sneezing and a discharge from the nose. Fortunately it is easily treated with appropriate antibiotics and most dogs recover without having any long-lasting problems.

The parainfluenza virus on its own can cause a mild form of kennel cough, but if caught alongside *Bordetella Bronchiseptica* it can cause a severe form of the disease.

Puppies initially obtain antibodies from their mother's milk in the first few days of their life, so as long as their mother was vaccinated, the puppies will have some protection against diseases for their first few weeks. These antibodies prevent vaccines from being effective and so it is advised that puppies receive their first vaccine from six to eight weeks of age after the maternal antibody levels have dropped. A second vaccination is then needed at ten to twelve weeks to ensure full immunity. A puppy should not be allowed outside, or anywhere he may come into contact with unvaccinated dogs, until a week after the vaccinations, allowing his immunity time to develop.

Booster vaccinations normally happen annually after the puppy's initial vaccinations, but there is much debate about whether annual vaccinations are required, given the low risk of catching the disease. There is also an argument over whether vaccinations share a link with other health problems caused by over-vaccinating.

It is true that vaccines against viruses stimulate a longer-lasting protection, and many vets recommend vaccination against distemper, parvovirus and hepatitis be carried out every three years after the initial booster. However, as the protection from the primary course of immunization does not last for ever against viruses such as parainfluenza and leptospirosis, booster vaccinations are advisable. Vaccines against bacterial infections (such as kennel cough) may only last for a matter of months and so it is important to vaccinate your dog against kennel cough every time he goes into boarding kennels.

If you are unsure about the need for booster vaccinations or vaccinations for specific diseases, speak to your vet, who will be able to best advise you on suitable vaccines, based upon the local disease prevalence, your lifestyle and your dog.

# CHAPTER 11

# SIGNS OF ILLNESS

## DIARRHOEA

Diarrhoea is usually a sign of an upset stomach and is a response to a dietary choice. Goldens are nearly always looking for something edible and will happily tuck into the faeces of some animals such as horses or cows.

Normally diarrhoea is not serious and a day or two on bland food such as cooked chicken and rice will settle the stomach. If, however, your dog is also vomiting, lethargic, has blood in his stools and appears to be in pain, or the diarrhoea lasts longer than forty-eight hours, seek veterinary help as it may be caused by something more serious. If your dog has eaten a stone, this also requires veterinary attention as it will not necessarily pass through and can be fatal if left untreated.

## VOMITING

Vomiting, like diarrhoea, is a sign of an upset stomach.

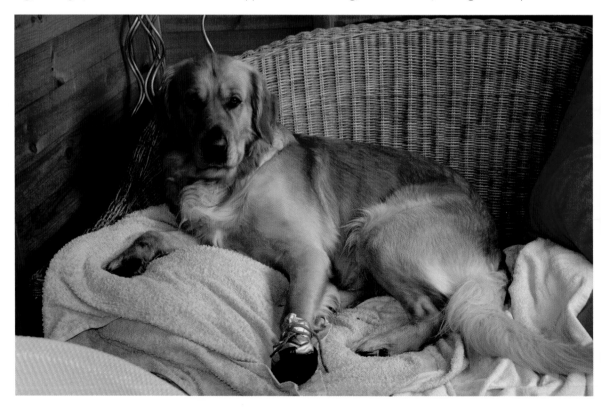

*You can purchase boots specifically designed for dogs to protect a hurt foot.*

It can also be a natural result of issues such as car sickness, the eating of excessive amounts of grass, hunger (usually when only bile is vomited), and over-eating.

If your dog is sick only once, there is normally nothing to worry about, and he should be given a bland meal and a small supply of water, and normal activities can be carried out. If, however, there is repetitive vomiting, blood in the vomit, other medical signs such as convulsions or diarrhoea, or your dog appears in pain, seek veterinary assistance as it could be a response to various illnesses and diagnosis needs to be carried out as quickly as possible.

*Your vet will be able to carry out an eye examination to ensure your dog's eyes are healthy and his vision is not impaired.*

## LAMENESS

Lameness is a change in gait and movement; if your dog is lame, he may stagger or limp when he walks, put less or no weight on one leg, or refuse to stand up. Lameness is often the response to pain in either the leg or the back. It is common when the dog has hurt a foot, be it cut or sprained, and other signs will include licking the foot or lifting it up when standing. If your dog limps, the pain is likely to be further up the leg and may be related to the joints; there is often some inflammation with this type of injury. Veterinary attention should be sought for any lameness which causes pain or inflammation or lasts more than a few hours.

## EYE DISCHARGE

Occasional and morning eye discharge is normal and should be wiped away with a clean cloth. Should any discharge contain pus or blood, veterinary attention should be sought immediately. Any knocks to the eye, or if the eye is swollen or closed, should also be checked by a vet.

## NASAL DISCHARGE

Dogs should have moist, cool noses but that does not mean that a warm, slightly dry nose should cause alarm. A little watery nasal discharge is perfectly normal and can be wiped away with a clean, damp cloth. If the nose is very dry and cracked and/or the nasal discharge is thick with mucus or contains blood, seek veterinary attention as it could be a sign of a respiratory infection.

## EXCESSIVE DRINKING

Golden Retrievers have a thick coat and will drink more water in the summer months and after exercise to cool down. Very salty food will also lead to large amounts of water being drunk, but this will only be temporary and soon after the food is eaten. Excessive drinking is defined by large amounts of water being drunk throughout the day, regardless of food intake, exercise or weather conditions. You should always pay attention to the amount of water your dog drinks so you are aware if his thirst increases. Excessive drinking can be a sign of kidney disease or diabetes, so any increase of water intake should be taken seriously and veterinary advice sought.

## ABNORMAL BREATHING

Panting can be rapid in hot conditions and after exercise and is completely normal; allow your dog to cool down and rest until his breathing returns to normal. Nervousness and stress can also cause abnormal breathing, but are not commonly life-threatening. Abnormal breathing patterns that require immediate veterinary attention include excessive panting, wheezing, air sucking or loss of breath. Any of these signs should be considered an emergency as it may indicate a serious condition, airway obstruction or heart disease.

## COUGHING

The occasional cough should cause no alarm. However, elderly dogs with a cough should be seen by a vet to ensure is it not a sign of heart disease. When coughing is persistent, rasping in sound, causing breathing problems or is followed by mucus and/or vomit, then veterinary attention should be sought without delay. Early diagnosis and treatment will result in a quicker recovery. Coughing can be caused by a respiratory

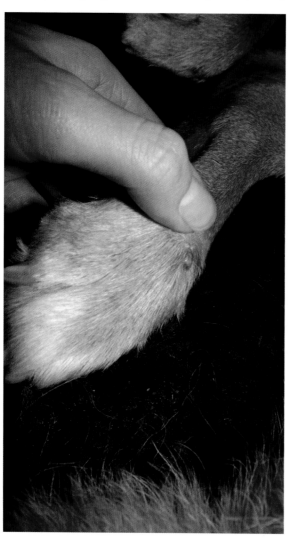

or heart problem, but is also associated with kennel cough.

## LUMPS

Finding a lump on your dog can be concerning and often raises the fear of it being cancerous. Lumps can occur at any age, but are common in Golden Retrievers in their later years and are normally nothing more than fatty deposits under the skin (lipomas) and generally cause no problems. They are not often removed as they generally do not affect your dog's behaviour, health or physical ability. An increase in lump size or any lump that affects your dog's comfort should be examined and possibly removed.

Don't assume that all lumps are lipomas, and any lump on your dog should be investigated by a vet. If necessary, the vet will take a small tissue sample of the lump to send to a laboratory for diagnosis.

Each case is different and lumps can be caused by many things. Non-cancerous lumps include lipomas, cysts, in-growing hairs and warts. There are also cancerous lumps that can be malignant or benign. Malignant lumps spread rapidly and can appear in any part of the body, whereas benign lumps stay in one place but can grow huge.

If the lump in question is deemed a tumour or the vet is suspicious of infection, it will be removed immediately and further tests carried out to ensure the problem has not spread. Treatment may also come in the form of radiotherapy and chemotherapy, which can be life-savers.

Many tumours, if caught early, can be removed and treated, and the dog will live a perfectly normal, happy and long life. Every lump found should be treated with caution and veterinary attention sought as early as possible.

*The small lump on the foot pictured here developed over a period of weeks and after investigation was classified as a wart.*

## LOSS OF APPETITE

Some dogs will lose and regain their appetite on occasion throughout their life and this is normally not of any concern. Elderly dogs can lose their appetite if they have gum disease or tooth decay, which will require dental treatment. Puppies get upset stomachs quite easily as they chew on pretty much anything they can get their teeth into, and loss of appetite may simply be due to an upset stomach and their appetite will be regained again by the next feed. Some fussy eaters may protest against eating unless a better dish is served, in which case speak to a food supplier for the most suitable mix for fussy eaters (try not to give in and serve leftovers every night for your dog).

Remember that no dog will starve himself, so if your dog has not eaten anything for more than one day, it is best to ask advice from your vet as the cause could be stress- or health-related and should be diagnosed as quickly as possible.

## EAR INFECTIONS

Ear infections are not uncommon in Golden Retrievers. The main cause of ear infections is a build-up of bacteria. Goldens simply adore swimming, but if water gets into their ears they can get infected. Seed heads are another culprit, as are ear mites. Dogs that suffer from allergies, such as to pollen, dust or moulds, frequently suffer ear infections. This is due to the inflammation that the allergies cause, allowing overgrowth of bacteria and yeast organisms.

Scratching or rubbing the ears and head shaking are the usual signs that your dog has an ear infection. The ear may be red and inflamed and/or have dark brown or black wax in the ear. Ear cleaning solutions suitable for dogs are an easy way to keep the ear clean. Simply squirt a couple of drops down the ear canal and massage the bottom of the ear from the outside (you should be able to hear a squelching sound); then,

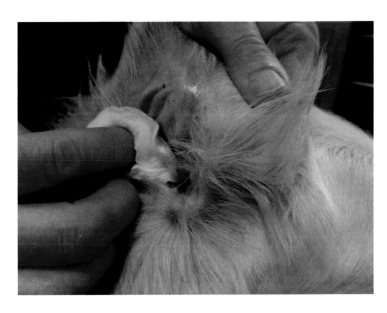

*Ears should be cleaned with a pad as shown and not with a cotton bud.*

using a cotton pad, wipe out any build-up of wax or dirt.

The ears should be cleaned regularly to keep out any infection and remove any moisture, as this can lead to the growth of micro-organisms. If your dog has an ear infection for more than twenty-four hours and is progressively getting worse, see your vet as if left untreated ear infections can cause more serious issues.

## ANAL SACS

The anal sacs, located on either side of the anus, empty a very small amount of anal gland fluid each time faeces pass through. On occasion the anal sacs do not empty properly and can fill with a fluid that gives off a particularly pungent smell, and can become infected. Some dogs will 'scoot' their bottom along the floor, trying to relieve the irritation, or will excessively lick the area, but the pungent smell is normally the first noticeable sign that the anal glands are full.

Soft stools are one reason why the anal sacs do not empty properly, so increasing the fibre content in your dog's diet will firm his stools and trigger the anal sacs into releasing the fluid.

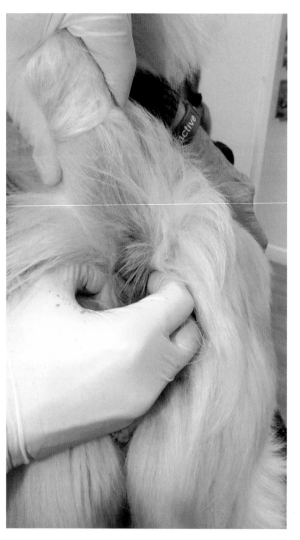

*Your vet will show you how to clear the anal sacs.*

Emptying the anal sacs can be done at home, but if you do not fancy trying this yourself, or are unsure, a vet will do it for you. If it is the first time your dog's anal sacs have filled with the fluid, visit your vet to ensure there is no underlying infection.

Emptying the sacs is a relatively simple thing to do. Wearing rubber gloves, first locate the sacs: if you imagine your dog's anus as a clockface, the sacs would be situated at 4 and 8 o'clock. Have someone hold your dog steady in the standing position, and gently hold the dog's tail up out of the way with one hand. With the other hand, gently place your forefinger and thumb on either side of and slightly below the anus. Full anal sacs will feel like two peas. Once you have found them, gently squeeze them in an upwards motion in the direction of the anus. Do not apply too much pressure; it will take several squeezes to remove the fluid, and you will know when the sacs are emptying as a fluid will be produced. Keep squeezing until there is no more fluid and the sacs are deflated. Ensure you wipe your dog's bottom so there is no fluid left.

If after several attempts no fluid comes out, consult your vet as too much squeezing can make the problem worse and even cause infection.

# CHAPTER 12

# HEREDITARY HEALTH

## HIP DYSPLASIA

Hip dysplasia is the abnormal development of the hips and is one of the hereditary conditions to which Golden Retrievers are susceptible. The degree of abnormality in a dog is indicated by a score for each hip, and the hip score is the total of those scores.

Each breed is given a mean score for hip dysplasia. The average score for a Golden Retriever is 18 (which could be a score of 9 per hip). The minimum hip score (per hip) is 0 and the maximum is 53. The lower the score, the less likely it is that hip dysplasia is present. It is important to remember, though, that other factors such as over-exercising can also cause hip dysplasia, and even having two parents with hip scores of 0 will not necessarily mean your dog will never get the disease. The hip scores do, however, provide assistance when you are buying a puppy or deciding to breed, and in the long term will help to reduce the number of dogs with this debilitating disease by increasing awareness of whether the parents are likely to pass on this problem.

To get the scores, a dog must have his hip joints x-rayed by a vet. The x-rays are sent to the British Veterinary Association, where it is examined by a panel of experts and a score given. The x-rays, with the scores, are then returned to the vet, who relays the information to the owner. A copy is also sent to the Kennel Club for

recording on the dog's details on the database. A hip score only needs to be done once in a dog's life.

Hip scoring can be done when the dog is over one year old and breeders are advised only to breed from dogs with hip scores below the breed average.

## ELBOW DYSPLASIA

Elbow dysplasia is the abnormal development of the elbow joint. As with hips, the elbows are x-rayed and given a score by the experts at the British Veterinary Association, and the results passed to the owner and the Kennel Club. The difference with elbow dysplasia is that the scoring is between 0 and 3, but only the higher grade is given as an overall grade. Again, the dog needs

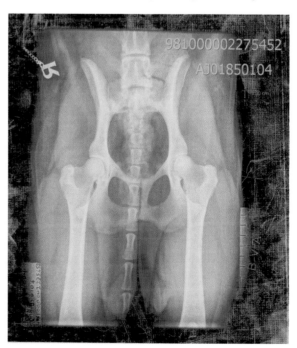

*A x-ray of a Golden Retriever's hips. The score for this dog was 0-0.*

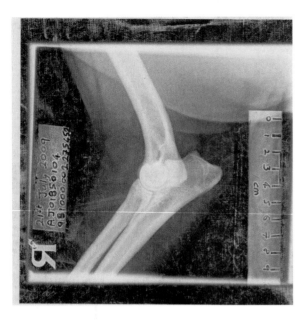

*An x-ray of the right elbow. The score was 0.*

to be over the age of one to have his elbow score done and breeders are advised only to use breeding stock with an elbow score of 0. As with the hip score, the elbow score only needs to be done once in a dog's life.

## EYE CONDITIONS

Golden Retrievers can inherit or develop several eye conditions. Eye schemes can be carried out to check if your dog has inherited or developed any of these conditions. This should be done on an annual basis, as problems can either develop over time or show no symptoms until later in life.

The eye scheme consists of a group of canine ophthalmologists, who examine the dog and look for clinical signs that will indicate whether the dog is affected by any of the eye conditions. If there are no clinical signs then the dog will be declared 'unaffected', but if there are signs of an eye condition he will be declared 'affected'. The results are passed back to the owner and to the Kennel Club for inclusion on the dog's details.

*Carrying out health tests is important for the health of future puppies.*

By screening dogs for these retinal diseases, breeders can make informed decisions about whether or not to breed from their dogs.

### Hereditary Cataract (HC)

HC is the clouding of the lens of the eye, which is caused by a mutation in the genes, which in turn causes a breakdown of the tissue. HC normally affects both eyes and results in the dog not being able to see clearly; in later stages it can cause blindness. Surgery is available to correct the lens, but it is often costly and not always effective. Cataracts are not always hereditary; they can also develop in the dog's later life or after an eye injury.

### Progressive Retinal Atrophy (PRA)

PRA is an eye condition which results in impaired vision or blindness. It results in the degeneration of the retina and comes in two forms, generalized PRA (GPRA) and centralized PRA (CPRA). GPRA is the more common condition of the two, but both are hereditary. GPRA results in the gradual loss of vision in both eyes due to the degrading of the retina cells that sense light. In CPRA the coating of the retina degrades at a much slower rate and normally affects older dogs, but ultimately leads to impaired sight. At present there is no treatment for PRA.

### Multi-focal Retinal Dysplasia (MRD)

Retinal dysplasia can be focal or multi-focal, and can be seen as streaks or dots in the eye. It is connected with folding of the retina, but in some cases it can be completely harmless and non-progressive. Retinal dysplasia in geographic form, which appears as irregular-shaped patches in the eye, can lead to the retina becoming partially or completely detached, causing blindness in that eye. Retinal dysplasia can be caused by a recessive gene or through infections, deficiencies or medical drugs. In most cases the cause is hereditary and puppies can be screened for MRD before going to their new homes.

Golden Retrievers can also be screened for the following eye conditions: Multi-ocular Defects (MOD), Congenital Hereditary Cataract (CHC) and Coloboma (C).

# CHAPTER 13

# FIRST AID

Prevention is always better than cure and with reasonable diligence, if you know your dog, how to care for him and what to look out for, most problems can be avoided. However, accidents do happen and knowing what to do can often save you and your dog a lot of suffering and trauma.

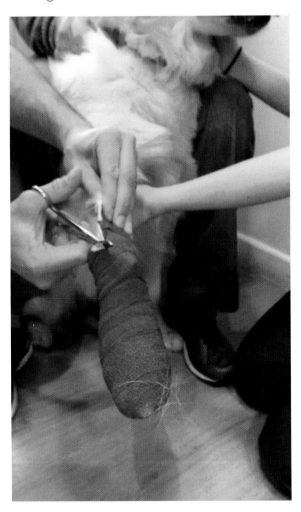

Most first aid is common sense, and the fundamental principles of first aid for humans will also apply to dogs. Having some knowledge of basic first aid will make you feel less helpless in emergency situations. In any emergency, take a deep breath and try not to panic. Time is of the essence and the first few minutes after an incident can be crucial to the survival of the victim (depending on the severity of the accident).

First, assess the situation and try to work out what has occurred. Do not, in any circumstance, put yourself in danger. Unless you are absolutely certain that you can handle the situation, send someone to summon professional help, in most cases a vet. Ensure that as much information as possible is provided, allowing

**Top Tip**

Try to keep your dog calm until veterinary attention can be sought, by limiting the number of people around him, talking to him soothingly, reducing any noise or light, and staying with him. Do not leave him alone at any time during a distressing situation.

*Ensure a suitable bandage is sourced as quickly as possible for large cuts. Unless advised otherwise, always allow your vet to remove bandages.*

**Top Tip**

Never use cotton wool directly on a wound as it will stick and leave traces of wool. If a first aid kit is not to hand, use a clean piece of cotton clothing or something similar to hold against the wound to stop the bleeding. If your dog has cut his foot, you can use a sock and a hair tie to encase the foot, to keep it clean until you get home.

the vet to assess the seriousness of the situation. If you are alone, summon help yourself before you do anything else, unless the patient is not breathing or has no pulse.

It is worth having your vet's phone number on your mobile phone for such instances. Unless it is absolutely vital, do not move the pet as you may cause more damage. Do not give him food or water, or try to lift or move his head in any way that could allow bodily fluids, blood or vomit to run back into the airway and potentially block it. Always comfort the dog by gentle stroking and talking to him all the time.

## BLEEDING

Cuts on the paw are one of the most common injuries with dogs. The treatment for bleeding is, however, much the same whichever part of the body is injured. Using a clean absorbent dressing, apply firm pressure to the wound to stem the flow of blood.

Arterial blood is bright red and comes out in spurts. A ruptured or cut artery is a life-threatening situation and continual pressure must be applied; if the blood soaks through the dressing, do not be tempted to remove it, but add an additional dressing on top and continue to apply pressure until veterinary help arrives.

## BURNS

Typical signs of burns or scalds are swelling, redness, singed fur and even fur coming away from the skin, blistering of the skin and open wounds. Before attending to your dog, ensure that the same thing cannot happen to you. For example, if your dog has chewed through an electric cable, be certain that the electricity supply has been turned off, preferably at the mains, before touching your dog or the cable.

Saturate the injured area with clean cold water, preferably under a convenient cold water tap or by using a showerhead if at all possible. In order to minimize the damage, you will need to keep this up for at least ten minutes and probably longer in order to ensure that the burn or scald is not continuing to damage the skin.

Never apply oils or creams as this will increase the severity of the injury. After at least ten minutes of running the wound under cold water, apply a light non-fluffy dressing, without placing any pressure on the area. Do not use cotton wool. Soaking the dressing in cold water will also help.

## CHOKING

Given the opportunity, most Golden Retrievers will attempt to eat almost anything relatively edible. Do not allow your dog to play with anything that is likely to get stuck in his mouth.

Should your dog start to retch and paw at his mouth, check for obvious signs of an obstruction. It is sometimes possible to gently remove the object by flicking it forward and out of the mouth, but take care not to get bitten in the process.

Remember your dog will be in great distress and quite possibly unable to control his natural reactions. An asthma attack causes similar problems to an obstruction in the airway, with the possibility of the animal beginning to turn blue in colour. All these situations require urgent veterinary attention. Reassure your dog until veterinary help is at hand.

*Sticks are notorious for causing choking as parts splinter off in the mouth.*

## COLLAPSE

A heart attack, epileptic fit, diabetes, accident, burn or exposure to extremes of temperature can often bring on shock, leading to collapse. Carry out the ABC procedure (airways, breathing and circulation) in order to keep your dog alive until the vet arrives. Loosen the dog's collar, open his mouth and gently pull the tongue forward to ensure the airway is open. Feel for a pulse either at the inside of the thigh at the join between leg and torso, under the armpit or on the wrist.

If you can't feel a pulse, start cardiac massage of the heart (see the road traffic accident section for details). Although this technique undoubtedly saves lives, it is very dangerous and great care must be taken to ensure that you do not damage your dog further. Only use this technique if you are absolutely certain that his heart has stopped. Ensure you continue monitoring your dog until veterinary help arrives.

## FITTING

Epilepsy and similar conditions are not uncommon in Golden Retrievers. If your dog has a fit, it is a traumatic experience for both animal and owner. Veterinary help must be obtained and suitable advice as to how to care for your dog should further fitting take place in the future.

**Top Tip**

It is not recommended that you try to move your dog should a fit occur, unless he is in danger of injuring himself. You may use pillows to hold against nearby objects, such as a table, to make sure he does not hurt himself on it. If a fit occurs while you are with your dog, stay calm, stay with him and call your vet after the fit has finished. Do not try to hold him still, or scream or run off for help. A fit may only last a few seconds, so your dog will be very confused and restless when he comes round and he will need you to be present to reassure him. Then you can seek help.

Typical symptoms of fitting are drawn-back lips, glazed eyes, foaming at the mouth and flailing limbs. If possible, loosen your dog's collar, cover him with a blanket and make him as comfortable as possible. Do not leave him until professional help arrives.

## HEATSTROKE

Never leave your dog (or any other pet) in a car during hot weather. Dogs pant to lose heat rather than sweat through their skin, which means they will suffer grave problems if left in too much sun or heat without the provision of shelter, shade and drinking water. Dogs that sunbathe or go outside in hot weather should have a high factor sunscreen applied to their noses, the pink tips of their ears and their underbellies to help prevent sunburn.

*Avoid walking your dog in the midday heat during the summer months to reduce the risk of heatstroke.*

Keep an eye on sun lovers; the classic signs of heatstroke are panting, frothing at the mouth and eventual collapse. Try to notice the early warning signs and remove him from the sun and into the shade well before the problem becomes serious. Wipe the pet's mouth with a clean wet cloth and sponge down his entire body with cold water or wrap him in wet towels. Additionally, improvise a fan and rapidly (without causing him to panic) cool him down until professional help arrives.

Never throw buckets or cups of cold water over your dog, or push him into a river, pond or other water source as you will almost certainly send him into shock. All cooling actions should be gentle and soothing.

---

**Top Tip**

To reduce the risk of heat stroke, avoid walking your dog in the midday sun. Goldens have very thick coats and overheat easily, so in the summer months opt for early morning, late afternoon or early evening walks. Take plenty of water with you on long walks and always take a mobile phone.

---

## POISONING

Pets can suffer poisoning in a variety of different ways, involving many different common household substances, in addition to venom from snakes, toads and insects. Household items such as paint, bleach, chemicals of varying types, weed killer and rat poison should be kept out of your dog's reach.

If consumption does occur, typical symptoms of poisoning include breathing difficulties, orientation problems, pawing at the mouth, dribbling, convulsions and eventual collapse. Telephone your vet immediately and ask for immediate attention. Tell them which substance (or likely substance) has caused the problem and if at all possible take a sample with you. Unless the vet has instructed you to do so, do not give your dog a drink (especially not milk), or attempt to make him vomit.

If your dog has been doused with a substance such as bleach or acid, completely wash him with a weak soapy solution to reduce the risk of absorption through the skin. Keep washing until you are sure there are no traces left, then gently dry him either with a towel or with gentle heat from a hairdryer. There is a high risk of shock so try to keep him calm and warm until you get veterinary assistance, which is absolutely necessary in these circumstances.

*See also* the table of poisonous plants at the end of this chapter.

## ROAD TRAFFIC ACCIDENTS

Road traffic accidents are most pet owners' worst nightmare and they are quite possibly among the most traumatic situations you will ever find yourself in. Assess the situation first and ensure you do not put yourself or others at risk; you will be of no use to your pet if you are also on your way to hospital. Where possible, get assistance to stop or divert the traffic.

Call your vet straight away (or a local vet if you are away from your home area). Do not move your dog unless it is vital to his safety. If you are forced to move him, use a blanket, coat or other similar item as a stretcher and carry him between two people, as Golden Retrievers are not the lightest breed of dog. Once you know it is safe, try to reassure your dog by talking gently to him and see if you get a response. If he does respond, look for injuries (*see above* for cuts and other injuries). Even if he is apparently uninjured, he will undoubtedly be suffering from shock and should be kept warm and reassured until a vet arrives.

If your dog is showing signs of aggression but does not appear to have any breathing problems, approach from behind his head and muzzle him with a bandage, scarf, sock or something similar that can be gently tied.

If your dog is not responding, check his airway and breathing by watching to see if his chest rises and if you can feel his breath on the back of your hand. Check for a pulse either at the inside of the thigh at the join between leg and torso, under the armpit or on the wrist.

*The heart is located where the elbow meets the chest. In this picture, the person's hands are over the dog's heart.*

If the airway is clear but you can hear or even feel air leaking out of a wound, gently press a dampened pad to the wound to seal it, thus reducing the risk of a collapsed lung.

If the airway is not clear and your dog is not breathing but he does have a pulse, lay him on his right side, to reduce pressure on the heart. (Your dog's heart is located on the left side of his body, roughly where the elbow meets the chest if you bring the elbow back towards the chest.)

Clear the airway by pulling your dog's tongue forward to remove any mucus, vomit or blood. Align your dog's head with his back and then tilt it back a little. Cupping both hands around your dog's mouth, and ensuring no air can escape, place your mouth over your dog's nostrils and mouth and blow five quick breaths. Watch for a rise in the chest, and wait two or three seconds to allow the air to escape. Continue breathing in, watching for the rise and waiting for the air to escape until the vet arrives.

If your dog is not breathing and does not have a heartbeat, perform cardiac massage along with the artificial respiration (as described above). Place your hand on your dog's chest where the heart is located. Locking your fingers and your elbows, press down gently but firmly fifteen times in ten seconds. Then

**Top Tip**

Remember: fifteen compressions to one breath and one squeeze. Continue the compressions until help arrives, as it can make a huge difference in saving a dog's life. Always have your vet's phone number on your mobile phone as a contact, and do ask them if they have a 24/7 service for emergencies and, if so, what the number is for that also.

go back to artificial respiration, but blow in one breath rather than five.

To achieve circulation of the blood around the heart, slip one hand underneath the dog nearer the abdomen, place the other on top and squeeze.

## STINGS AND BITES

Stings and bites can cause serious injuries. Victims may suffer an allergic reaction and require urgent veterinary treatment. Usually the first you know of this type of injury is the obvious initial distress and swelling of the area.

Cooling a swelling caused by a bee sting with bicarbonate of soda will help, whereas a wasp sting can be better treated by bathing in vinegar. Obviously if the injury is caused (or could have been caused) by a venomous creature (such as a snake), the administration of the appropriate antidote is of the utmost urgency. Any swelling in the region of the throat requires immediate treatment or the consequences may prove fatal.

## BASIC FIRST AID KIT

Keeping a basic first aid kit in your home and in your car is useful for responding to common injuries and emergencies. Pet first aid kits are available and provide the basics especially suited for their needs, but you can ensure that everyone in the family is looked after by buying a first aid kit for human use and adding a few extras for your dog.

Your first aid kit should contain:

- tweezers (useful for thorns in pads)
- self-cling bandages (these do not stick to fur)
- scissors, preferably round-ended
- adhesive tape
- antiseptic cream
- soft, lint-free, sterile pads
- bicarbonate of soda (for bee stings)
- vinegar (for wasp stings)
- socks (to put over dressings on limbs and tails)
- eye bath and wash
- a muzzle or something that can act as a muzzle (long socks work just as well)
- a spare nylon lead
- pen and paper
- disposable gloves
- vet details (phone number and address).

In addition to the items listed above, ensure you add anything recommended by your vet to cover your dog's specific requirements. Remember always to check the use-by dates of items and replace those that have expired. Lastly, always keep your first aid kit out of reach of children and pets.

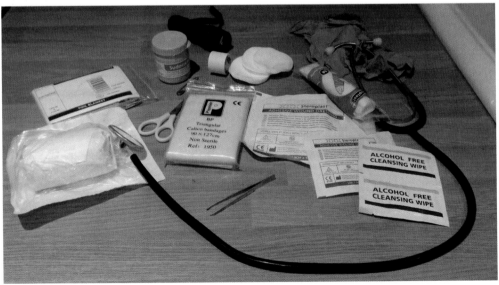

*Other items useful to have in your first aid kit include a stethoscope, a thermal blanket, a variety of bandages and a torch.*

# POISONOUS PLANTS

| Plant Name | Possible Symptoms (if known) |
| --- | --- |
| Aconite: roots, foliage and seeds (*Aconitum* species) | Toxic if eaten, causing nausea and vomiting. May also affect cardiac function – increased heart rate. |
| African violet: leaves (*Saintpaulia ionantha*) | |
| Aloe vera | Diarrhoea. |
| Amaryllis: bulbs (*Hippeastrum* species) | Upset stomach, hyperactivity, lethargy, coma, shock. Can be fatal. |
| Angels' trumpets (*Brugmansia* species) | Toxic if eaten, causing nausea and vomiting. |
| Angel wings (*Caladium* species) | Upset stomach, oral irritation, asphyxiation, tremors, seizures, loss of balance. Can be fatal. |
| Apple: seeds (*Malus* species) | Seeds contain cyanide. Varied toxic effects. |
| Apple leaf croton | |
| Apricot: kernels (*Prunus armeniaca*) | Kernels contain cyanide. Can be fatal. |
| Arborvitae (*Thuja* species) | Harmful if eaten in quantity. May cause a skin allergy. |
| Arrow grasses (*Triglochin* species) | |
| Asparagus fern (*Asparagus setaceus*) | Contains a wide variety of poisons resulting in a range of symptoms. |
| Autumn crocus (*Crocus speciosus*) | Vomiting, nervous excitement. May cause dermatitis. |
| Avocado: fruit and pith (*Persea americana*) | Diarrhoea, vomiting, laboured breathing. Can be fatal. |
| Azalea (*Rhododenron occidentale*) | Nausea, vomiting, depression, difficulty breathing and coma. Can be fatal if eaten in large enough quantities. |
| Baby's breath (*Gypsophila paniculata*) | |
| Barilla: leaves and stems (Salsola soda) | |
| Bird of paradise: seeds (*Strelitzia reginae*) | Gastrointestinal tract affected by the plant toxins. |
| Bittersweet (*Celastrus angulatus*) | Toxic if eaten, causing nausea and vomiting. |

| Plant Name | Possible Symptoms (if known) |
| --- | --- |
| Bleeding heart: foliage and roots (*Dicentra formosa*) | Poisonous in large amounts, contains convulsants. May also cause dermatitis. |
| Bluebell (*Hyacinthoides*) | Harmful if eaten in quantity. |
| Box: leaves (*Buxus sempervirens*) | |
| Boxwood: leaves and twigs (*Hebe odora*) | Upset stomach, heart failure, excitability or lethargy. May also cause dermatitis. |
| Bracken (*Pteridium aquilinum*) | Thiamine deficiency, acute haemorrhagic syndrome, blindness, tumours. |
| Broom (*Cytisus* species) | |
| Buckeyes: nuts and immature growths (*Aesculus* species) | Harmful if eaten in quantity. |
| Burning bush (*Kochia scoparia*) | Toxic if eaten, causing nausea and vomiting. May cause a skin allergy. |
| Buttercup (*Ranunculus* species) | Juice may severely injure digestive system. May also cause dermatitis. |
| Caladium (*Caladium* species) | |
| Calico bush (*Kalmia* species) | Harmful if eaten in quantity. |
| Calla lily: leaves (*Zantedeschia* species) | Harmful if eaten in quantity. |
| Caper Spurge (*Euphorbia lathyris*) | |
| Cardinal flower (*Lobelia cardinalis*) | |
| Castor bean: leaves and seeds (*Ricinus communis*) | May cause dermatitis. A single Rosary Pea or one/two Castor bean seeds can be fatal. |
| Ceriman (*Monstera deliciosa*) | Causes diarrhoea and oral irritation if eaten. May cause dermatitis. |
| Chenille Plant (*Acalypha hispida*) | |
| Cherry: kernels (*Prunus* species) | Kernels contain cyanide. |
| Cherry laurel (*Prunus laurocerasus*) | Harmful if eaten in quantity. |

| Plant Name | Possible Symptoms (if known) |
|---|---|
| China Berry (*Melia azedarach*) | |
| Chinese evergreen (*Aglaonema*) | |
| Christmas rose: leaves and roots (*Helleborus niger*) | Harmful if eaten in quantity. |
| Chrysanthemum: leaves and stems (*Chrysanthemum* species) | May cause dermatitis. |
| Cineraria (*Senecio* species) | |
| Clematis (*Clematis armandii*) | Gastrointestinal tract and nervous system affected by plant toxins. May cause dermatitis. |
| Cocoa husks or mulch | Similar toxic effects to that of chocolate – hyperactivity, increased heart rate. Can kill if enough is eaten. |
| Corn cockle: seeds (*Agrostemma* species) | Harmful if eaten in quantity. |
| Corn plant (*Dracaena* species) | |
| Crocus (*Anemone* species, *Colchicum autumnale*) | |
| Croton (*Codiaeum* species) | |
| Crowfoot (*Anunculus* species) | |
| Crown vetch (*Coronilla varia*) | |
| Cuckoo pint (*Arum maculatum*) | Toxic if eaten, causing nausea and vomiting. May cause a skin allergy. |
| Cycads (*Encephalartos* species) | |
| Cyclamen (*Cyclamen* species) | Gastrointestinal tract affected. Convulsions and paralysis. |
| Daffodil: bulbs (*Narcissus* species) | Nausea, vomiting, diarrhoea. May also cause dermatitis. Can be fatal. |
| Daphne (*Daphne* species) | Gastrointestinal tract and kidneys affected. May cause dermatitis. |
| Datura (*Brugmansia* species) | |
| Deadly nightshade (*Atropa belladonna*) | Toxic if eaten, causing nausea and vomiting. |

| Plant Name | Possible Symptoms (if known) |
| --- | --- |
| Delphinium: seeds and young plants (*Delphinium* species) | Harmful if eaten in quantity. |
| Devil's fig (*Solanum hispidium*) | Harmful if eaten in quantity. |
| Dieffenbachia (*Dieffenbachia* species) | Causes diarrhoea and oral irritation if eaten. May cause dermatitis. Tremors, seizures, loss of balance, asphyxiation. Can be fatal. |
| Dragon tree (*Dracaena* species) | Vomiting and diarrhoea. |
| Dumb cane (*Dieffenbachia amaena*) | Causes diarrhoea and oral irritation if eaten. May cause dermatitis. Tremors, seizures, loss of balance, asphyxiation. Can be fatal. |
| Dwarf morning glory (*Convolvulus tricolor*) | Harmful if eaten in quantity. |
| Easter lily (*Lilium longiflorum*) | Especially poisonous to cats. |
| Echium (*Echium* species) | Harmful if eaten in quantity. May cause a skin allergy. |
| Elder: leaves, root and bark (*Sambucus* species) | |
| Elderberry (*Sambucus canadensis*) | Nausea and vomiting. |
| Elephant ears (*Bergenia* species) | Intense burning, irritation and swelling of the mouth and throat. If tongue swells enough to block air passage, can be fatal. |
| English ivy: berries and leaves (*Hedera helix*) | Gastrointestinal tract affected. May cause dermatitis. |
| European spindle (*Euonymus europaeus*) | Harmful if eaten in quantity. |
| False hellebore: roots, seeds and leaves (*Veratrum album*) | Toxic if eaten, causing nausea and vomiting. |
| Flannel flower (*Phylica plumosa*) | Harmful if eaten in quantity. |
| Flax (*Linum usitatissimum*) | Harmful if eaten in quantity. |
| Foxglove: leaves and seeds (*Digitalis* species) | Toxic if eaten, causing nausea and vomiting. |
| Fritillary (*Fritillaria* species) | |
| Fruit salad plant (*Monstera deliciosa*) | Causes diarrhoea and oral irritation if eaten. May cause dermatitis. |

| Plant Name | Possible Symptoms (if known) |
|---|---|
| Gaultheria (*Gaulthera mucronata*) | Harmful if eaten in quantity. |
| Geranium (*Geranium* species) | |
| German ivy: berries and leaves (*Delairea odorata*) | Gastrointestinal tract affected. May cause dermatitis. |
| German primula | Toxic if eaten. May cause skin allergy. |
| Glory lily (*Gloriosa superba*) | Toxic if eaten, causing nausea and vomiting. |
| Golden chain: seed capsules (*Laburnum*) | Toxic if eaten, causing nausea and vomiting. |
| Granny's bonnets (*Aquilegia vulgaris*) | Harmful if eaten in quantity. |
| Heavenly bamboo (*Nandina domestica*) | |
| Heliotrope (*Heliotropum arborescens*) | |
| Hellebores (*Helleborus* species) | |
| Hemlock (*Tsuga* species) | |
| Henbane (*Hyposcyamus niger*) | Toxic if eaten, causing nausea and vomiting. |
| Hibiscus (*Hibiscus* species) | |
| Holly: berries (*Ilex* species) | Upset stomach, tremors, seizures, loss of balance. |
| Horse chestnut: nuts and leaves (*Aesculus hippocastanum*) | Harmful if eaten in quantity. |
| Hurricane plant: bulb (*Monstera deliciosa*) | Varied toxic effects. Causes diarrhoea and oral irritation if eaten. May cause dermatitis. |
| Hyacinth: bulbs (*Hyacinthus orientalis*) | Harmful if eaten in quantity. May cause a skin allergy. |
| Hydrangea (*Hydrangea* species) | |
| Iris: roots (*Iris* species) | Severe digestive upset. May cause dermatitis. |
| Ivy (*Hedera helix*) | Harmful if eaten in quantity. |
| Jack in the pulpit (*Arisaema* species) | Causes burning to the mouth. Can cause hallucinations. |
| Japanese spindle (*Euonymus sieboldianus*) | Harmful if eaten in quantity. |

| Plant Name | Possible Symptoms (if known) |
| --- | --- |
| Japanese yew (*Taxus* species) | |
| Jerusalem cherry: immature growths (*Solanum pseudocapsicum*) | Gastrointestinal tract affected. May cause dermatitis. |
| Jessamine: berries and sap (*Cestrum* species) | Digestive disturbance. Gastrointestinal tract and nervous system affected. Can be fatal. |
| Jimson weed (*Datura stramonium*) | Abnormal thirst, distorted sight, delirium, incoherence, coma. Can be fatal. |
| Jonquil, bulb (*Narcissus* species) | |
| Juniper (*Juniperus* species) | |
| Kalanchoe (*Kalanchoe* species) | Depression, rapid breathing, teeth grinding, ataxia, paralysis. |
| Kale (*Brassica oleracea*) | Haemolytic anaemia, goitre, possible reduced fertility. |
| Kingcup (*Caltha palustris*) | Harmful if eaten in quantity. |
| Laburnum: leaves and seeds (*Laburnum anagyroides*) | Toxic if eaten, causing nausea and vomiting. |
| Lantana (*Lantana camara*) | Toxic if eaten, causing nausea and vomiting. |
| Larkspur: young plants and seeds (*Delphinium* species) | Digestive upset, nervousness, depression. Cardiovascular system affected. May cause dermatitis. Can be fatal. |
| Laurel (*Prunus* species) | Harmful if eaten in quantity. |
| Lenten rose (*Helleborus orientalis*) | Harmful if eaten in quantity. |
| Leopard lily (*Belamcanda species*) | Toxic if eaten, causing nausea and vomiting. May cause a skin allergy. |
| Leyland cypress (*Cupressocyparis leylandii*) | Harmful if eaten in quantity. May cause a skin allergy. |
| Lily (*Lilium* species) | Harmful if eaten in quantity. |
| Lily of the valley: leaves, flowers and roots (*Convallaria* species) | Toxic if eaten, causing nausea and vomiting. |
| Lily of the valley bush (*Pieris japonica*) | |

| Plant Name | Possible Symptoms (if known) |
| --- | --- |
| Lobelia (*Lobelia* species) | Harmful if eaten in quantity. May cause a skin allergy. |
| Locust (*Robinia* species) | Nausea and weakness. |
| Lupin: leaves and seeds (*Lupinus* species) | Harmful if eaten in quantity. |
| Mallow (*Lavatera* species) | Harmful if eaten in quantity. |
| Maple Tree (*Acer* species) | |
| Marijuana (*Cannabis sativa*) | Contains hallucinogens. |
| Marsh marigold (*Caltha palustris*) | Harmful if eaten in quantity. |
| May apple: apples, roots and foliage (*Podophyllum peltatum*) | Severe diarrhoea. Nervous system affected. |
| Meadow rue (*Thalistrum delavayi*) | Harmful if eaten in quantity. |
| Mezereon (*Daphne mezereum*) | |
| Milkweed (*Ascepias syriaca*) | Harmful if eaten in quantity. May cause a skin allergy. |
| Mistletoe: berries (*Phoradendron flavescens*) | Gastrointestinal tract affected. May cause dermatitis. If eaten by a puppy, a few berries can be fatal. |
| Monkshood (*Aconitum napellus*) | Digestive upset and nervous excitement. Cardiovascular system affected. |
| Morning glory: seeds and roots (*Ipomea* species) | Harmful if eaten in quantity. |
| Moroccan broom (*Cytisus battandieri*) | Harmful if eaten in quantity. |
| Mother-in-law's Tongue: leaves (*Dieffenbachia amaena*) | Causes diarrhoea and oral irritation if eaten. May cause dermatitis. Tremors, seizures, loss of balance, asphyxiation. Can be fatal. |
| Mountain laurel (*Kalmia latifolia*) | Harmful if eaten in quantity. |
| Naked ladies (*Colchium* species) | Toxic if eaten, causing nausea and vomiting. |
| Narcissus: bulbs | Nausea, vomiting, diarrhoea. May cause dermatitis. Can be fatal. |
| Needlepoint ivy: berries and leaves | Gastrointestinal tract affected. May cause dermatitis. |

| Plant Name | Possible Symptoms (if known) |
|---|---|
| Nerine (*Nerine bowdenii*) | |
| Nightshades (*Solanum* species) | Intense digestive disturbances. Can be fatal. |
| Oak: foliage and acorns (*Quercus* species) | Affects kidneys. Symptoms appear after several days. |
| Oleander (*Nerium oleander*) | Affects the heart, produces severe digestive upset, extremely poisonous. May cause dermatitis. Can be fatal. |
| Onion (*Allium* species) | Causes anaemia. Onions should not be fed to dogs in any form. |
| Paspalum: seeds (*Paspalum* species) | Dermatitis. |
| Pasque flower (*Pulsatilla vulgaris*) | Harmful if eaten in quantity. |
| Peace lily (*Spathyphyllum*) | Gastrointestinal tract affected. May cause dermatitis. |
| Peach: stones and leaves (*Prunus persica*) | Contain cyanide. |
| Pencil cactus (*Opuntia leptocaulis*) | |
| Peony: roots (*Paeonia* species) | |
| Peruvian lily (*Chlidanthus fragans*) | Harmful if eaten in quantity. May cause a skin allergy. |
| Philodendron: leaves (*Philodendron* species) | Causes diarrhoea and oral irritation if eaten. May cause dermatitis. |
| Pineapple broom (*Cytisus battandieri*) | Harmful if eaten in quantity. |
| Poinsettia: leaves, stems and sap (*Euphorbia pulcherrima*) | Diarrhoea, abdominal cramps, delirium. Sap can cause irritation and, if rubbed in eyes, blindness. May also cause dermatitis. |
| Poison hemlock (*Conium maculatum*) | Nervous system affected. May cause dermatitis. Can be fatal. |
| Poison ivy: leaves, bark and fruit (*Toxicodendron radicans*) | Poisonous. Can cause severe blistering dermatitis if coming into contact with skin. |
| Poison oak: leaves, bark and fruit (*Toxicodendron*) | May cause dermatitis. |

| **Plant Name** | **Possible Symptoms (if known)** |
|---|---|
| Poison sumac (*Toxicodendron vernix*) | Poisonous. Can cause severe blistering dermatitis if coming into contact with skin. |
| Pokeroot (*Phytolacca americana*) | Toxic if eaten, causing nausea and vomiting. |
| Pokeweed (*Phytolacca americana*) | Toxic if eaten, causing nausea and vomiting. |
| Poppy: unripe seedpod (*Papaver* species) | Harmful if eaten in quantity. |
| Potato: green skin and sprouts (*Solanum tuberosum*) | |
| Prickly poppy (*Argemone mexicana*) | Harmful if eaten in quantity. |
| Primrose: leaves (*Primula vulgaris*) | Upset stomach. May cause dermatitis. |
| Privet: leaves (*Ligustrum* species) | Harmful if eaten in quantity. |
| Ragwort (*Senecio* species) | Causes kidney failure and liver damage which is irreversible. Minute doses fatal, often wrongly diagnosed. |
| Raisins | Cause kidney failure. Can be fatal. |
| Rape (*Brassicus napus*) | Haemolytic anaemia, blindness, damage to nervous system, digestive disorders, breathing problems. |
| Red-ink plant (*Phytolacca americana*) | Toxic if eaten, causing nausea and vomiting. |
| Rhododendron (*Rhododendron* species) | Nausea, vomiting, depression, difficulty breathing and coma. Can be fatal. |
| Rhubarb: leaves (*Rheum* species) | Large amounts of raw or cooked leaves can cause convulsions and coma. Can be fatal. |
| Rosebay (*Rhododendron aureum*) | Toxic if eaten, causing nausea and vomiting. |
| Rose periwinkle (*Catharanthus roseus*) | Harmful if eaten in quantity. |
| Rue (*Ruta graveolens*) | Toxic if eaten, causing nausea and vomiting. May cause a skin allergy. |
| Sago palm (*Cycas revolute*) | Can be fatal. |
| Savin (Juniperus sabina) | Harmful if eaten in quantity. |

| Plant Name | Possible Symptoms (if known) |
|---|---|
| Schefflera (*Brassaia actinophylla*) | Harmful if eaten in quantity. May cause a skin allergy. |
| Silkweed (*Asclepias* species) | Harmful if eaten in quantity. |
| Snowdrops (*Galanthus* species) | |
| Solomon's seal (*Polygonatum*) | Harmful if eaten in quantity. |
| Spider plant (*Chlorophytum* species) | May cause vomiting and salivation. |
| Spruce Tree (*Picea* species) | |
| Spurge (*Euphorbia* species) | Harmful if eaten in quantity. May cause a skin allergy. |
| Squill (*Scilla* species) | Harmful if eaten in quantity. |
| Starflower (*Smilacina stellata*) | Harmful if eaten in quantity. |
| Star-of-Bethlehem: bulbs (*Ornithogalum* species) | Harmful if eaten in quantity. |
| St Johns Wort (*Hypericum perforatum*) | Harmful if eaten in quantity. |
| String of pearls/beads (*Senecio rowleyanus* or *herreianus*) | |
| Sweet pea: stem (*Lathyrus odoratus*) | Harmful if eaten in quantity. |
| Swiss cheese plant (*Monstera deliciosa*) | Causes diarrhoea and oral irritation if eaten. May cause dermatitis. |
| Taro vine (*Monstera deliciosa*) | Causes diarrhoea and oral irritation if eaten. May cause dermatitis. |
| Tiger lily (*Lilium*) | Especially poisonous to cats. |
| Tobacco plant: leaves (*Nicotiana*) | Harmful if eaten in quantity. |
| Tobira (*Pittosporum tobira*) | |
| Tomato: green fruit, stem and leaves (*Lycopersicon lycospersicum*) | |
| Tulip (*Tulipa* species) | Harmful if eaten in quantity. May cause a skin allergy. |
| Umbrella plant (*Schlefflera* species) | Toxic if eaten, causing vomiting and diarrhoea. |

| Plant Name | Possible Symptoms (if known) |
|---|---|
| Varnish tree (*Toxicodendron vernicifluum*) | Poisonous. Can cause severe blistering dermatitis if coming into contact with skin. |
| Walnut: green hull juice (*Juglans nigra*) | |
| Water dropwort, Hemlock (*Oenanthe crocata*) | Rapid-onset violent convulsions. Can be fatal. |
| Water hemlock (*Cicuta maculate*) | Violent painful convulsions. Can be fatal. |
| Wax tree (*Toxicodendron succedaneum*) | Poisonous. Can cause severe blistering dermatitis if coming into contact with skin. |
| Weeping fig (*Ficus* species) | |
| Wild cherry tree: twigs and foliage (*Prunus avium*) | Gasping, excitement, prostration. Can be fatal. |
| Windflower (*Anemone* species) | Harmful if eaten in quantity. |
| Wistaria: pods and seeds | Nausea, repeated vomiting, stomach pains, severe diarrhoea, dehydration and collapse. |
| Wolfsbane (*Aconitum septentrionale*) | Toxic if eaten, causing nausea and vomiting. |
| Woody nightshade | Toxic if eaten, causing nausea and vomiting. |
| Yarrow (*Achillea* species) | |
| Yew: berries and foliage (*Taxus* species) | Dizziness, dry mouth and mydriasis develop within one hour, followed by abdominal cramping, salivation and vomiting. Can be fatal. Foliage is more fatal than berries. Death can be sudden, without warning or symptoms. |

Poisonous Plant list reproduced by courtesy of Dog's Trust, charity number 227523

# CHAPTER 14

# SHOWING

## WHY SHOW?

Everyone believes their dog to be the most beautiful dog of all, and many would like the chance to show him off. Showing your dog is a great activity to take part in; it strengthens your bond with your dog, enhances training, creates a wonderful community where like-minded people can get together and is fun. You do not need to know lots about showing to take part. The notion that only a few people can be involved and that showing is a closed group is a misconception. In fact, showing offers a great day out for your dog, where he can socialize with lots of other dogs in a relaxed atmosphere, and gives you the opportunity to meet and become friends with other Golden owners. And, of course, without its history of showing, the Golden Retriever as a breed may never have become the popular breed it is today.

Showing can become highly addictive and absorbing, especially if you have a competitive nature. It can also extend into breeding, to better the breed, continue a rated bloodline and perhaps produce the next winning dog. Showing can quite easily become an exciting and all-consuming hobby. Some enthusiasts may want to go on to make a living from their dogs, become judges or key influential people in the dog world.

*ShCh Thornywait Billie Jean.*
(Photo by courtesy of Liz Molnar)

## START SHOWING

Once you have made the decision that you wish to show your pedigree Golden Retriever, the first step is to ensure he is registered in your name on the Kennel Club breed register. If your dog is not registered with the Kennel Club in the correct ownership, your entry will not be accepted, other than at fun or companionship shows.

Before you decide to show your dog it is wise to go to a show beforehand to get a feel for it, see the dogs in action and gain an understanding of what the judge is looking for. It is a great chance to meet other like-minded people and ask lots of questions. If you intend to buy a puppy for showing, it will also give you a chance to meet lots of people who are successful with their Goldens in the show ring.

Dogs cannot enter shows until they are a minimum of six months old but should begin training before then. Your dog will not automatically know how to be a show dog and attending ringcraft classes will give you all the skills you need on how to present your dog at a show.

Ringcraft classes are run by dog trainers or people who have extensive experience in dog showing. You may need to do some research to find a suitable training school that offers these classes near you. Ringcraft classes are not only a great way to learn how to present your dog, but also build your Golden's sociability with other dogs and people as there will be potentially hundreds of both at some shows.

Once you feel confident that you and your dog are ready to try out your first show, you need to find a suitable show.

Golden Retrievers are part of the Gundog group, which is made up of different breeds that were used to assist in finding and retrieving game, predominantly birds. Gundogs also come in groups: Retrievers (to which Goldens belong), Flushers (mostly Spaniels) and Pointers (Pointers and Setters, and the like). The other groups are Working, Hound, Pastoral, Terrier, Toy and Utility.

There are several different types of show that can be entered. There are fun shows and companion shows, which are normally held in your local community and consist of classes such as 'the most handsome dog' and 'dog with the waggiest tail'. These classes are open to all dogs, whether Kennel Club registered or not. For all the following types of show, they do need to be registered.

*SweCH Floprym Rivaldo.*

Single Breed shows, as the name suggests, are only open to one breed, and normally only last a day, while Group shows are bigger and all dogs from the Group can enter. General shows are among the biggest and consist of classes for all the groups of dogs.

Limited shows are breed-specific and take place all around the country, held by regional clubs. They are run by the respective breed clubs, of which you must be a member to enter the show.

Open shows are open to all levels (beginners and experienced) and breeds, and generally have a relaxed atmosphere about them. They are a great starting point for those entering into showing for the first time. Premier shows are likewise open to all levels, but being placed at a Premier show will qualify your dog for Crufts.

Championship shows are open to all exhibitors but the competition is much greater as the reward for being

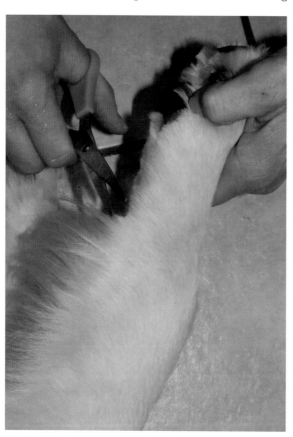

*The feet should be trimmed to show the definition.*

placed in a championship show is a Challenge Certificate (CC) and a qualification for Crufts. If your dog wins three CCs, he will become a show champion, which is one of the highest achievements in the showing world.

A list of licensed shows can be found on the Kennel Club's website, Fosse Data or the breed club websites. For some shows you have to belong to a breed club to enter. When you have decided which show you wish to attend, you will need to ask the secretary of the show for the schedule and apply to enter classes in the show (you can apply for more than one class).

Shows take place all around the country so ensure you are prepared for a long day by bringing everything you and your dog might possibly need. Shows often take place in a field, so ensure you are wearing suitable footwear. Many handlers dress to present, and often don casual suits or similar attire.

When you reach the showground, allow your dog to relieve himself and settle into the environment before expecting him to enter the ring. If it is your or your dog's first show it will all be very exciting, so get there as early as possible to look around, find out where your class is being held and watch other classes. This will give you an idea of what the judge is looking for, and also provides an opportunity to see how other handlers present their dogs.

General rules on a show ground include:

- dogs should be kept on the lead at all times;
- no harsh treatment or punishment towards any dog will be accepted;
- any fouling should be picked up;
- no bitches may be mated at a show;
- you should not try to interfere with another dog in the show ring; and
- you should never question the decision of the judge.

## GROOMING FOR THE SHOW RING

If you are entering a show, you will want to present your Golden at his very best. A thorough grooming should be done a day or two before the show, with the finishing touches only at the showground. Goldens, in

*IntCh Thornywait Gift to Floprym.*

comparison to other breeds, need less preparation in terms of grooming before a show, but you should still spend some time enhancing your dog's best features for the day.

Start by bathing your dog to remove any stains. When he is fully dried, brush him all over, ensuring all the knots and tangles are gone. Using thinning scissors to give a more natural result, trim the hair at the front of the neck, and lightly trim the hair behind and along the ears. Tidy the hair around the feet to give a neat shape and his tail feathering.

Your dog should look natural in the ring, and freely show off his qualities. To achieve this look, many handlers use a show lead rather than a standard collar and lead. A show lead is a thin slip lead which, when placed at the top of the neck, near the head, encourages your dog to lift his head high in the show ring. Using a show lead gives an elegant and natural look.

## AT THE SHOW

At a dog show the judge will be judging each dog against the Kennel Club's Breed Standard for Golden Retrievers. As you enter the ring you will be asked to stand your dog in a line with the other contestants. Goldens should stand in a natural position, with their head held high and their feet squarely in line.

Each entry in turn will be asked to come forward for inspection by the judge. The dog should be standing for this presentation and the judge will run their hands along your dog's body and look at his teeth. It is wise to practise with strangers handling your dog before entering a show as your Golden must tolerate inspection by the judge.

After the hands-on inspection, the judge will ask you to trot your Golden anti-clockwise around the arena in an almost triangle shape. Your dog must be on the inside of you, so the judge has an unobstructed view of him. Your dog should be moving with ease at a decent speed and should not change his gait (break into a canter or slow down to walk). It is worth practising trotting around with your dog in front of crowds of people as your dog must stay focused on what he is doing and not be distracted by things going on around him or put his nose to the floor. The judge will be looking for style and conformation that most accurately matches the breed standard.

After you have trotted around the arena, the judge may want to look at your dog again, or will otherwise ask you to return to the line-up. Once all the entries have been inspected and trotted around individually, you may be asked to trot around again as a group and then stand for the final judgement.

The judge will point to the individuals who have been placed, with third place being called first, then second and finally first place. No matter the result, it is a matter of courtesy to thank the judge.

For many people the end goal of showing is to qualify for Crufts, one of the largest dog shows in the world. It was founded by Charles Cruft, a showing enthusiast, in 1891 as an exhibition to show off the best of the breeds. Now run by the Kennel Club, it has developed significantly over the years.

Crufts is held over three days at the NEC in Birmingham every March, and alongside the showing rings boasts hundreds of trade stands selling everything and anything for and about dogs. Crufts is open to the public and makes for a fantastic day out, whether you are interested in showing or not. The Southern Golden Retriever Display Team attends the event every year and puts on a fantastic display of Goldens, showing them at their best.

The main events are held in the main arena and over the three days there are numerous activities including agility, flyball, heelwork to music and Gamekeeper classes; there are also competitions and displays. The Best in Show class, the ultimate showing dream, is held on the final day.

The showing at Crufts is organized at various levels in a hierarchical system. You may enter your dog in classes based on age and gender. If you win your class, the next stage is to compete against the opposite gender of the same class; if you win again, you can enter best of breed. The classes are held in rings in the halls designated for specific breeds, but if you win Best of Breed, your next class will take place in the main arena.

Here the Best of Breeds compete against other breeds in the same group, to win Best of Group. Here your Golden will be up against other Retrievers, Spaniels, Setters and Pointers. Once the Best of Group is chosen, the winners of each group go on to compete for Best in Show and Reserve Best in Show.

The prize for winning Best in Show at Crufts is a small cash prize (£100) and a replica of the coveted solid silver Keddall Memorial Trophy, which is permanently held at the Kennel Club's headquarters in Clarges Street, London. The real prize, though, for winning Best of Show is pride.

Since the beginning of Crufts, the Gundog group has had the highest number of winners of Best in Show, but the Golden Retriever is yet to receive the glory.

Showing your dog is an exciting activity and winning a class at a show fills any owner with a huge amount of pride. Remember, though, no matter what place your dog gets in a show, no rosette or cup can match the special bond you have with your Golden. The real prize is that you get to take the best dog home.

# CHAPTER 15

# OTHER ACTIVITIES

## TAKE PART

Golden Retrievers really come into their own when they are given a job to do. It doesn't necessarily have to be the job they were originally bred to do, as any activity that provides physical and mental stimulation will appeal to your Golden. Licensed activities that a Golden can take part in include field trials or Gundog working tests, but there are also more informal activities such as agility, flyball, obedience, heelwork to music and rally.

## AGILITY

Agility is growing in popularity because it is often the most enjoyable of the activities for both human and

*Golden Retrievers love having a job to do.*

dog and is a great form of exercise for both. It can be done simply for fun or on a more competitive basis at shows. In terms of competition, the Golden, although a quick and agile dog, will not be able to compete with the likes of German Shepherds and Border Collies, who excel at this sport. Agility for Goldens is more about the fun element for both handler and dog, as they will complete the course with accuracy but perhaps not speed.

Agility is essentially a timed obstacle course for your dog, and he must complete all the obstacles in the right order. It is a fitness and obedience challenge for both dog and handler as the two must work together to complete the course, with the handler always being one step ahead, ready to show the dog which obstacle is next and control his speed over it. There are up to fifteen obstacles, which include jumps, tunnels, weaving poles, see-saws, ramps, pause tables and hurdles. It is open to all breeds of dog and is categorized in three

sizes, small, medium and large, based on the height of the dog. There are seven grades, with grade one suitable for beginners.

To begin training your dog in agility, you can either set up an agility course in your garden at home (agility packs can be purchased from various internet sources) or attend an agility training school.

It is important that no puppy takes part in agility. Your dog must be a minimum of twelve months old before even beginning training. The jumps, walks and ramps can be extremely high and very dangerous for a puppy should he fall off, and can put a strain on his joints and bones while he is growing.

Whether you attend a training school or build an agility course at home, remember to start with the easy obstacles first, such as jumps. Your Golden will enjoy these and will be keen to do more. Introduce new obstacles that may be quite scary, such as the A-frame or see-saw, by gently encouraging your dog to explore

*You can even find agility obstacles out on a walk.*

it first. You can even make much smaller versions of these obstacles too.

Once your dog has practised with each of the obstacles and is comfortable tackling each one, you can start linking them together and picking up the pace. Staying in front of your dog enables you to guide him to the next obstacle. At the end of certain obstacles will be a painted (normally yellow) strip. On this strip your dog must wait or pause for at least a second.

To enter a licensed agility competition, your dog must be registered with the Kennel Club, either on the breed register or on the activity register. The dog must be over the age of eighteen months to take part in competitions. He will be measured to ensure he is entered into the correct size class (Goldens are almost always in the large category).

You can then enter a competition suitable for your grade. Competitions are run by clubs up and down the country. You need to gain points during the agility course to go up in grades. The types of competition vary but include:

- matches: these are open to members of a club only;
- limited shows: these limit numbers, breeds, members and so on;
- open shows: these, as the name implies, are open to everyone;
- premier shows: these are for qualifiers for Crufts or Olympia; and
- championship shows: these are the ultimate in agility, where handler and dog are competing for an Agility Certificate.

*An agility course set up at Crufts.*

Remember always to reward your dog when you have finished, even if he has not performed as well as you had hoped. Whether it is just for fun or you are competing, agility is a fun sport and should be enjoyable first and foremost for both handler and dog.

## FLYBALL

Flyball is another sport that is growing in popularity. It is a highly competitive event where a team of four dogs will compete against another team by running over parallel sets of jumps to reach the flyball box. Each dog must press the pedal on the flyball box to release a tennis ball. The tennis ball must be caught in mid-air before the dog runs back over the jumps. When the dog reaches the start/finish line, the next dog is released. The team that finishes first, with all balls returned, wins. The team that wins the best of three runs progresses to face the next team.

This activity is great fun for everyone, and takes great skill in training the dog to release and return the tennis ball quickly. Although this sport is dominated by Border Collies, your Golden will relish this activity and it will bring out his natural retrieving instinct. To take part in this sport you need to join a flyball team; a complete list of flyball teams can be found on the British Flyball Association website: www.flyball.org.uk.

## HEELWORK TO MUSIC

The title says it all. Dog and handler must perform a routine to a piece of music, lasting up to four minutes. The routine can consist of any number of tricks and the only boundary is your imagination. Goldens do very well in this sphere, as they have a natural desire to please their handler.

The basis of this activity is heelwork. Your dog must be able to walk closely to heel and be engaged with you, watching for every command and working with you. The choice of music is completely the handler's but should be appropriate to the chosen routine. Handler and dog will be judged on the content of the routine, the accuracy of the moves and their interpretation of the music. Judges want to see a routine that is choreographed in time with the music, and incorporates a variety of tricks and moves that flow with ease and show off the handler's and dog's skill.

There are limited training schools that will train in this sport, but there are a number of clubs that can be joined and shows are held throughout the country.

## OBEDIENCE

Goldens make excellent dogs for competitive obedience. Their natural desire to work and their train-

*Obedience takes practice to perfect. Your Golden should respond instantly to commands.*

ability make them a favourite for this activity. Once you have mastered basic obedience, you can continue to advanced training and enter obedience competitions where you and your dog will carry out a set of exercises that will be judged.

Both dog and handler are judged for the accuracy and precision of each exercise. For beginners, the exercises include heelwork, recall, stays and common positions such as sit and down, but as you advance up the levels the exercises become increasingly difficult, with the highest level requiring skills such as distance control, retrieve, send away and scent detection. Each exercise is marked according to its execution, and you need to achieve certain marks to move up to the next level of competition.

The initial levels of competition class are:

- Introductory, for handlers and dogs who are new to obedience, and allows for the use of treats to help the dog to focus;
- Pre-beginners: this is suitable for those who have won in the introductory class. Once you have won a pre-beginners class, you are not able to enter another class at this level.
- Beginners: once you have won more than two beginners classes, you are no longer eligible for this class;
- Novice: more experienced handlers bringing on a young dog often start at this level.

More intensive competitions for successful handlers and dogs start with Class A, followed by Class B and finally Class C, the highest level of competition. There are three levels within Class C: Open, Limited and Championship. To enter a championship class, you must have won a Class C Open class.

Obedience competition can be very rewarding for both handler and dog as it tests their skill, precision and control. Even if you decide not to compete in obedience, it is rewarding to advance your dog's training, so your Golden will be a credit to you everywhere you go.

## RALLY

One of the newest dog sports available, this involves you and your dog navigating your way around a course by following numbered signs. Each sign asks for a different exercise to be performed. Think of it as 'obedience meets agility'. You do not need to stop between exercises, but must continue until you complete the course, which will consist of up to fifteen exercises. Handlers are allowed to walk the course and look at the exercises before the competition begins.

For beginners, dogs are walked through the course on a lead and encouragement is allowed to assist with the exercises, but at more advanced levels dogs are required to be off the lead. The exercises consist of heelwork and control exercises, such as stop and sit, sit and stay, sit and lie down and then stand, with higher level exercises including recall over jump, turn from dog and call to heel.

There are six levels to compete in, with beginners starting at Level 1. Points are deducted rather than awarded. Each handler and dog starts with 200 points and points are deducted for any mistakes made during the course. Qualifying will require a score of at least 170 on three occasions.

Given the obedience aspect, Goldens make excellent dogs in this sport as it rewards advanced obedience training and brings in an element of fun.

## WORKING TRIALS

Working trials were originally – and sometimes still are – seen as the equivalent of police dog training but it is now a competitive sport. Working trials always take place outside and throughout the year. Trials are not restricted to German Shepherds, and any breed can enter, but it is physically very demanding on both handler and dog. Golden Retrievers can do exceptionally well in some elements of working trials.

A considerable level of training is required to complete working trials. Your dog will be tested on his intelligence, fitness and obedience through the various sections. These include nosework, agility and control.

### Nosework

This is a search and track exercise, whereby the dog must follow a laid track, which is often over half a mile

*Part of nosework requires the dog to follow a laid scent track.*

long across fields and rugged landscapes, and must seek out objects that are placed along the track and also search for and retrieve objects that are thrown out along the way. Goldens, being bred to retrieve, excel at and enjoy this section of a working trial.

### Agility

For this section your dog must clear three agility obstacles: a 3ft hurdle, a 6ft wooden fence and a 9ft long jump, with only two attempts permitted for each obstacle. Goldens are heavy-set dogs and some may struggle with this more athletic section, but do not let that put you off as a fit Golden may surprise you with his capabilities. Do bear in mind, however, that if you teach

your dog to climb and jump such heights, it can cause issues should your dog choose to jump over the fence in your own garden.

### Control

This section requires your dog to display obedience in heelwork, stay, retrieve, bark on command and steadiness to gunshot.

To begin training your Golden for working trials, you can join a club, as well as go on training courses and training weekends held throughout the country. It is hard work, but very rewarding. As with agility, your dog must be at least eighteen months old before entering a competition and should be at least one year old before beginning the more strenuous aspects of training.

Trials can take place anywhere in the country, so be prepared to travel long distances to competitions and ensure you pack everything you and your dog require. In addition, they may take place over several days, so you may need to stay away from home. This can incur considerable costs, in both time and money, so be sure to check the trial schedule, as you may find that all your tests are on one day or split over several days.

Ensure your dog is well enough to compete on the day. Trials can be very testing and physically demanding, and pushing your dog when he is not well can be detrimental to his health and well-being. You can withdraw from an exercise at any point.

Once you have decided to enter a competition, you will need to start at the lowest level and work your way up through the ranks of:

- companion dog;
- open and championship Utility dog;
- open and championship Working dog;
- open and championship Tracking dog;
- open and championship Patrol dog.

To progress in rank a dog must gain at least 70 per cent marks in each exercise and at least 80 per cent overall. The highest achievement is to be a Working Trial Champion; to achieve this accolade the dog must win two certificates at Tracking Dog and/or Patrol Dog level under different judges.

# CHAPTER 16

# FIELD TRIALS

## TRAINING A WORKING GOLDEN RETRIEVER

Whether you choose a traditional working type or show type, your dog must be capable of working all day out in the field in any terrain and any weather. Training should start as a puppy and you will need to be dedicated to training your dog to bring out the best in him and get him ready for the field.

Hobby trainers and those whose dogs are also pets will want their dogs to be able to serve multiple purposes, both fitting into the family lifestyle and being able to work in the field. It is not impossible to achieve, but it will require discipline and a lot of training and dedication. For companion dogs, training for field trials often begins with everyday commands and progresses to specific training for the field. In particular, you will need to train him to hunt and retrieve. Goldens are bred for this job, so a lot of what he is learning will come naturally.

Training can begin as early as four to five months old for a confident puppy, but more normally at seven to eight months old. Training should start with the retrieve; practise retrieving with a young puppy using an old glove, bundled-up socks or something similarly soft and interesting. A Golden puppy will not need much encouragement to go out and pick up the item, but bringing it back to you needs practice. Always train

*Goldens are eager to please and love to work.*

*Expect to lose some feathers during training.*

a young puppy quietly; do not be in a hurry to take the item from the puppy, and never snatch the item from his mouth: this will lead to a rough delivery and a hard mouth. By asking slowly and carefully for the picked-up item, you are teaching your dog how to deliver with ease and with a soft mouth.

Practice should be occasional. Training a young puppy for the field does not require hours and hours of solid training. It is far better to practise little and often to keep a puppy's attention.

The next stage of puppy training is asking for the retrieve. Throw out an item and point to it as he goes to retrieve it. You may say 'fetch', but bear in mind that in the field you are required to be as quiet as possible and your dog should retrieve on signal alone.

The final basic puppy training for field work is the drop. As your puppy brings the item back, give a command in the form of a hand signal to deliver the item into your hand. Always reward a young puppy

for delivering an item, so he gets something out of the retrieve as well.

Once the basic retrieve is mastered, you can continue your training by asking your puppy to wait before retrieving. This can take a while for young eager Goldens to understand. If your puppy lurches ahead before you have asked him to, put him on a lead before throwing the item out, and then ask him to fetch it. It is also worthwhile asking your puppy to stay while you fetch the item, to teach him that he only fetches on command (and he will not be allowed to retrieve someone else's game in the field!). With a solid retrieve in place, the next level of training includes perfecting sitting, lying down and staying to command, walking to heel and recall at the whistle.

As a working dog comes to age (around twelve months), many trainers start with retrieving a dummy and doing basic hunting across a variety of terrain, including water. To start with, train your Golden to pick up and retrieve canvas dummies, before moving on to fur or feather dummies; these are often weighted to mimic game. Before moving on to real game, your Golden will need to produce a concise pick-up with these items and return instantly to you with the dummy or game, moving quickly and cleanly across the terrain, and perhaps clearing a hurdle.

The first time you move on to cold game (already deceased), you may find your Golden is so over-whelmed that he does not return as quickly with the game as normal, or he may even take it away for himself. To overcome this, throw out the game relatively close to you, so you have better control. With practice comes perfection. The hardest retrieve of all is with warm game (either only just deceased or still alive but wounded). Start with deceased warm game and move on to easy 'runners' (wounded and likely to be moving). Your dog may pull out a few feathers or damage the bird as he tries to pick it up, but any attempt should be rewarded; a clean pick-up can be mastered later on.

The retrieve training should be advanced at a level suitable for your dog; no two dogs learn at the same rate and it is far better to take your time and really perfect each stage than to rush it and try to get out in the field before your dog is ready.

As he perfects the retrieve from a distance, you can

begin to increase the degree of difficulty; when you are out on a walk, drop the dummy and walk on, then send him back to find it. You can also hide the dummy and then send your dog off to seek it out. All these training techniques can be done on a normal daily walk, but remember to keep training short for the best results, and try to find different terrains to walk across.

Your dog will also be required to become accus-tomed to the sound of a firing gun. As with training for fireworks or any other loud and unexpected noises, make the noise quiet to begin with, drowning it out and distracting your dog with something else, like his dinner. Once he is quite happy to ignore the sound, you can begin to reduce the drowning-out noise until you are left with a pure gunshot. With sufficient training, even gun-shy dogs can be taught to accept loud noises; it is normally pet dogs who only hear it occasionally that develop this fear. By exposing your dog to loud noises more regularly, he will be desensitized.

Training a gundog can take many years, and even then, no amount of training can really prepare you or your dog for the real thing. The excitement of his first field trial is often so intense for a young dog that you may find him 'doing his own thing' rather than listening to you. To reduce this likelihood, it is worth gaining as much 'real life' experience as possible before entering field trials.

## LIFE IN THE FIELD

Golden Retrievers are at home and in their element in both field trials and working tests. Field trials resemble a shoot, and are designed to test your Golden's work-ing ability. Field trials are firm favourites with gundog owners, as they offer the chance to show the breeds at their very best and doing what they were bred to do.

If you love of the countryside and its traditions, field trialling is a very rewarding and enjoyable sport for both human and dog. It is worth learning all there is to know about field trials before deciding to start, certainly at

*Life in the field can involve a fair amount of waiting.*

competition level. There are numerous country shows and game fairs throughout the year that are worth attending to meet other gundog enthusiasts and to watch field trials and working tests at first hand. There may also be seminars and demonstrations at such events, which provide a great opportunity to speak to those already heavily involved in the sport and ask for advice or information.

If you intend to buy a Golden Retriever to take part in field trials, you will stand a better chance if your dog is of working type. Working bloodlines are bred specifically for the field and the resulting dogs are different from the more common show type in both looks and, quite often, temperament. Dogs from some show bloodlines display little interest in hunting, and are bred specifically for showing or as companions only. That does not necessarily mean, however, that show types cannot succeed in field trials or cannot be trained as gundogs.

The lifestyle of a working dog will vary from home to home. If you do decide you want to have several work-ing dogs and work them in the field annually and take part in competitive field trials, you will need to decide whether to have them kennelled or living in the house. Working dogs are often kennelled, living outside all year round and let out for training, working, exercise, feeding, etc.; such dogs generally do not take a central part in the family home and are first and foremost working dogs.

Dogs that live in kennels have a sole purpose and their life is focused on working in the field, with household manners and companion commands not taking precedence. Living in this way allows you and the dog to focus on and hone the important skills that will prepare him for a life in the field.

Joining a field trial society has many benefits, as there will be numerous training opportunities and such groups often hold members' competitions which will develop your and your dog's skills in ability, obedience and technique. Your dog will also need to learn how to work with other people and dogs around. The only

*The show-type Golden Retriever can make an excellent working dog with the right training.*

way to enter a field trial competition is by joining a field trial society; several hundred field trials and gundog working tests are held during the year but these often get fully booked very quickly. Once you have joined a field trial society, do go to trials just to watch. It will give you a chance to see what the trial entails, to watch the ability of the competition and to speak to top gundog trainers.

## GUNDOG WORKING TESTS

A gundog working test is the first competition to enter. It is ideal for those new to the sport and/or for young gundogs still in training. Unlike a field trial, it does not involve shooting game; dogs are instead required to pick up a dummy.

There are three different tests available, for Spaniels, HPR (Hunt, Point and Retrieve) dogs and Retrievers. Goldens will obviously be in the retriever group,

where they will be tested on their hunting ability and the speed and directness of their approach to find, pick up and retrieve a dummy. The judge will mark your dog for the following:

- a fast and accurate retrieve;
- the level of control when the dog is off the lead;
- control on the beating line;
- waiting at a peg;
- hunting for seen dummies;
- hunting for unseen dummies;
- retrieving from water;
- retrieving from the other side of an obstacle (a hurdle to jump);
- steadiness while the handler collects the dummy.

The judge will also take into account the level of quietness of instructions from handler to dog.

Unlike other intensive activity sports, dogs under the

*The Golden Retriever's calm nature makes them excellent gundogs.*

age of twelve months are permitted to enter gundog working test competitions in the puppy class, but your dog must not wear a collar of any kind or be on a lead during the trial.

Once you have entered several gundog working tests, you may feel ready to progress to field trials. These require a higher level of training, as the dogs will be expected to retrieve over longer distances and in much more difficult terrain.

## FIELD TRIALS

Your dog must, of course, be steady to gunshot and able to retrieve only on command. As field trials are conducted in real shooting environments, your dog will be expected to retrieve game wherever it should fall, and retrieve both dead and wounded game. Wounded game should be retrieved first and dispatched immediately. Once he has located the game, your dog should be as direct as possible and go for a clean pick-up (where he does not put the game down and pick it up again). He should deliver the game straight back to the handler, where the judge will examine the bird for signs of a hard mouth. This is done by checking the ribs for any breakage caused by picking up. Goldens have very soft mouths and excel in delivering a clean pick-up on the game.

There are different classes that can be entered and they consist of puppy stakes, all-aged stakes, novice stakes, open stakes and championship stakes. Awards or certificates of merit are given to those who are placed first, second, third and fourth. Winning any of these will entitle your dog to a stud book number, which will be registered with the Kennel Club and your dog entered into the stud dog register.

To qualify as a Field Trial Champion (FTCH), your Golden must be placed first in a Retriever Championship, win two firsts in 24-dog open stakes, win a first in a 24-dog stake and a first in a 12-dog open stake, or win three firsts in 12-dog open stakes.

# CHAPTER 17

# BREEDING

## SHOULD YOU BREED?

There are an increasing number of owners who want their bitch to have puppies either because she is a bitch and she can, or because it is 'a beautiful thing to behold', but this ideology can lead to irresponsible breeding. It is important as a breeder to ask yourself why you want to breed. Do you want to raise the standard of breeding? Do you want a puppy for yourself?

Is your bitch of such an incredible temperament that you wish to produce puppies that may be similar to her? Are you hoping to improve the breed by producing happy, healthy puppies? Is there a demand for your bitch's pups? Do you want you or your family to behold the beauty of birth? Or are you in it for the money?

Breeding for monetary reasons is not sensible. If this is the main purpose for breeding, it is likely that

*Golden mum with her puppies.*

the necessary time and expense needed to rear a litter will not be spent; moreover, despite what many people think, having a litter of puppies is not going to make anyone rich. Looking after the bitch before, during and after the pregnancy, covering vet bills, rearing the puppies, registering them and finding them suitable homes all costs a great deal more than many might think.

A pedigree, Kennel Club-registered Golden Retriever puppy would normally cost on average £500–£700, with more prestigious bloodlines achieving over £1,000. As a large breed, a bitch can often have around ten puppies in a litter. Totalling up these figures often sparks a desire to breed, but in fact the costs of preparation, mating, birth, rearing and selling of the puppies can actually cost thousands, so the end reward is not a cash gain.

Poodle crosses are becoming more and more popular, and these 'designer dogs' sell for a very high price due to the demand for them; at the same time, the price for purebred Golden Retrievers is decreasing. Goldens are still a very popular breed and huge numbers of puppies are born every year, which means there is no real 'demand' for more Golden puppies. Some Golden puppies may not find a home at eight weeks old and the breeder must be prepared to look after their puppies until they find suitable homes for them. It is a sad truth that some breeders become so desperate to sell their puppies that they allow them to go home with anyone, whether the new owners are suitable or not.

A high number of unwanted puppies often get dumped at rescue centres. In these circumstances it is clear that the breeder did not think carefully enough about the implications of having a litter before allowing their bitch to be mated, or perhaps they were hoping to make a quick buck from the puppies but then found they could not be sold.

Some breeders of Golden Retrievers breed purely for the love of the breed, or they hope to breed for a better future for Goldens, or they have a desire to help others, perhaps by donating a puppy to become an assistance dog. Donating a puppy has many rewards, and gives a great sense of pride from knowing that your puppy is going to make a difference to someone's life and you will be able to hear how he progresses and get updates throughout his life. Some charities like to select their puppy and will visit him several times, as well as asking for regular updates and providing guidance on what they expect from you as the breeder. You may be asked to follow some instructions and terms for donating a puppy, such as agreeing to handle the puppy daily, beginning some house training and keeping records. It is important to understand fully what is entailed before donating a puppy, so there are no misunderstandings further down the line.

Breeding is also extremely demanding. Puppies require a lot of supervision, especially when they reach about four weeks of age. From the day they are born it is a constant round of cleaning up after them, feeding them, playing with them, making sure they do not hurt themselves or start any bad habits. There will be sleepless nights, destruction and a lot of mess. If you work full-time it is not advisable to breed as bitches need close supervision before, during and after whelping. Whelping can sometimes last twenty-four hours, and so it is vital that your time can be flexible around the date your bitch is due. At the same time, though, it is one of the most exciting and fulfilling experiences. If you are prepared to put in the effort and time to do it all properly, the reward will be great. You will have raised beautiful, happy and healthy pups that will bring joy to their new owners, and you have provided them with the best possible start in life.

## WHERE TO START

If you are still set on breeding from your Golden, you must decide what kind of breeder you are going to be. Will you be breeding from multiple dogs? Will you breed more than five litters a year? Will you be a hobby breeder or make it a career choice? Anyone who wants to breed as a business must be licensed with the local authority. The Kennel Club has set up the Assured Breeders scheme to promote good breeding practice; it is accredited by UKAS (the United Kingdom Accreditation Scheme) and is recognized as providing a high standard of breeding. Thus potential owners can be confident that an Assured Breeder is the best point of contact for purchasing a healthy, well-adjusted puppy.

*Golden puppies in a basket.*

There are requirements that a breeder must follow to join the scheme:

- all breeding dogs must be registered with the Kennel Club;
- the puppy registration certificate must be passed on to the new owner of any puppy sold;
- any endorsements placed on the puppy's registration must be explained;
- they must follow the official policy on the maximum number of litters, frequency of litters and the age of the bitch;
- permanently identify breeding dogs in the form of microchipping, tattoo or DNA profile;
- abide by the Golden Retriever health schemes;

- provide a puppy pack to all new owners giving advice on exercise, feeding, socialization, training, etc.;
- provide written advice on the puppy's worming programme;
- provide written evidence of any vaccinations the puppy has received;
- provide post-sale advice to the new puppy owner;
- provide a sales contract for each puppy;
- provide information on Golden Retrievers that may enhance the new owner's understanding of their chosen breed.

It is strongly recommended that Assured Breeders also ensure that their breeding facilities follow good practice, commit to helping (if necessary) with the rehoming of any dog throughout its life; and follow all relevant health screening recommendations for Golden Retrievers.

There are many benefits to breeders joining the Assured Breeders scheme, such as free puppy listing and use of the Assured Breeders logo, but the main benefit is to the dogs themselves through the recognition it offers to puppy buyers. New owners today are more aware than ever of health schemes, in-breeding and puppy farming. Where once puppies were purchased cheaply, with little thought as to how they had been brought up, there is now deep involvement from many organizations that are creating wider awareness on the health and welfare of puppies. New owners now want to know where their puppies come from and understand what practices have been put into place to ensure the very best has been done for them. The Assured Breeders scheme provides peace of mind

for new owners, and joining the scheme puts registered breeders a step ahead of other breeders.

To join the scheme, an application form needs to be filled out and sent to the Kennel Club. The fee for joining the scheme is £20, plus a membership fee of £45 annually (figures accurate as of 2015). You will be inspected before being allowed to join the scheme, so it is vital that you apply well in advance of even planning a litter, and you should inform the Kennel Club when you plan to have a litter so the inspection can be planned accordingly. The inspector will be a reputable Regional Breeder Assessor (RBA). In applying to join the scheme, you are agreeing to allow the RBA to visit your premises and carry out an inspection. RBAs are often highly experienced breeders themselves and are trained by the Kennel Club in the inspection process. Every Assured Breeder will be visited every three years by an RBA.

The inspection can take up to two hours and the

*Mum, puppies and daughter from a previous litter enjoy some time outside.*

RBA will be looking for signs that you as a breeder comply with the Assured Breeders scheme criteria. Two main areas are covered: canine management, and facilities and documentation. The first part consists of questions designed to demonstrate your knowledge and understanding of breeding practices and you will be asked various questions about your dogs, such as how many you own, and where they live and sleep. They will want to know about your dogs' daily routine, exercise and diet. They will then move on to questions about the proposed litter, such as where the puppies will be raised and what steps you have already taken in planning the litter.

The RBA will need to see the results of any health tests that have been carried out and will want to look around your premises, especially at the areas where your dogs are kept and where the puppies will be raised.

Finally, the RBA will want to see a puppy pack, which should contain a copy of all the paperwork that would be supplied in a pack for a new owner. They will also want to check your dog's registration details to ensure the Assured Breeders scheme requirements are being met.

It can be quite nerve-wracking having your premises inspected and being asked multiple questions about your dogs, but the inspections are not designed to make a breeder fail, but to ensure the high level of breeding standards are met. You may ask the RBA as many questions as you like, and the RBA may go over any of their findings with you.

If, for whatever reason, you fall short of the standards required and you are asked to make improvements, there is normally a period of time in which you may provide evidence of improvement. In the worst case scenario, where the inspection has not been passed and membership of the scheme is refused, you will be required to wait three years before applying again.

You do not have to join the scheme to display good breeding practices. It is not a club for the breeding elite, and many breeders who are not part of the scheme actually go above and beyond the scheme's requirements.

If you find that breeding is for you and you wish to be recognized as a 'best breeder', the Kennel Club, supported by Our Dogs, runs an annual Breeders' Competition. This gives breeders the opportunity to show off their knowledge and their breeding stock. To enter the competition, you need three or four dogs that were bred by you to be present at the show you are entering. (You do not need to own the dogs, but you must have bred them.) If you have three or four suitable dogs lined up, you will then need to order a Breeders Competition Record Book, which can be purchased from the Kennel Club. The record book is currently

*Inspections should not be feared; they are there to ensure breeding success.*

*Young puppies sleeping together.*

(January 2015) priced at £1.50 and contains information on how to enter the competition, plus the fields that need to be completed after each stage. It is your responsibility to ensure that your record book is kept up-to-date and accurate.

Breeders' Competitions are held at every championship show; you do not need to have CCs to enter the competition and different groups can be entered for the Golden Retriever class; there are also AVNSC (Any Variety Not Separately Classified) entries. Entries can be taken on the day and it is free to enter.

To actually enter the competition, you will need a team consisting of the three or four dogs that you bred, plus a handler for each dog (which could be the owners of the dogs). Once you have a team and enter a class, you will be competing against other breeders for Best Breeder in Breed and Best Breeder in AVNSC; the winners of these will go on to compete for Best Breeder in Group. Gaining a place in Best Breeder in Breed, AVNSC and Group will all gain points, as shown below:

- Best Breeder in Breed/AVNSC class – 3 points
- Second place in Best Breeder in Breed/AVNSC class – 2 points
- Third place in Best Breeder in Breed/AVNSC class – 1 point
- Best Breeder in Group – 4 points
- Second place in Best Breeder in Group – 3 points
- Third place in Best Breeder in Group – 2 points
- Fourth place in Best Breeder in Group – 1 point.

Points accumulated throughout the year are entered into your record book, and must be registered on the Our Dogs website (www.ourdogs.co.uk/kcbreeders). The top fifty breeders who accumulate twenty-five or more points over the year will be eligible to qualify for the Crufts Final. Breeders should send off their record book to the Kennel Club, who will advise whether they qualify. If you do, you and your team will be able to compete for Best Breeder.

What it means to be Best Breeder (whether of Golden Retrievers or of other breeds) will mean different things to different people. It is a way of showcasing the best of the dogs you have bred, especially if they have done very well in the show ring, but it is also a chance to display your knowledge about breeding. The majority of Best Breeder winners are also Assured Breeders.

## HEALTH TESTS

Before breeding from your bitch, you must ensure she is healthy and free from hereditary conditions. The health tests for Golden Retrievers should be carried out before breeding from her. Many breeders get hip and elbow scores done when the bitch is around one-and-a-half years old. As a breeder, there comes a point

*Ensure your bitch is of the right temperament before deciding to breed.*

where you must consider what action to take should the health test results not be as expected or wished. If you find out that your Golden has a health problem and/or a hereditary condition, the responsible course of action is to not breed from her and to have her spayed to ensure the condition is not passed on. It can be disheartening to find out that your Golden's scores are not as good as you hoped. Many breeders are anxious about carrying out the tests, but they must be done for the sake of future puppies. If your dog has a condition, you do not want to pass that burden on to unknowing new owners, potentially causing distress for both owner and dog.

All the available health tests should be done before deciding to breed, to ensure you are not passing on a hereditary condition to the puppies. Another factor to take into account is the bitch's temperament. Many behavioural traits can be passed on by the parents, and if your bitch does not have a solid and sound temperament she should not be bred from. There are some behavioural traits that develop due to a lack of socialization and training, and these may disappear with correct handling; if so, it is more likely they were acquired rather than genetically inherited.

You may want to look at insuring your breeding bitch; it is completely optional but may provide some peace of mind. Some insurance companies will cover whelping bitches and the puppies for a number of weeks before they go to their new home. It can be costly, but some insurance companies and the Kennel Club do provide free puppy insurance for the first four weeks after puppies have gone to their new homes; it is worth asking around to find out what deals insurance companies are offering.

## SEASONS

Golden Retrievers can be bred from after the age of two years old. This is the optimum and recommended age for a first litter. A bitch will come into her first season as early as six months of age, but most start around the age of ten to twelve months and, depending on their cycle, will continue to come into season roughly every six to eight months afterwards. A bitch should not have litters from consecutive seasons, and you may find that

**Top Tip**

A false pregnancy can happen after a season during which the bitch has not been mated or has not been able to conceive. During a false pregnancy, the bitch shows signs of being pregnant, sometimes even lactating, and may display maternal behaviours. A bitch who has had one false pregnancy is likely to suffer with them every season. A mild false pregnancy should not require any intervention or medication. The behaviour will subside over time and can be sped up if toys and brooding objects are removed. Any production of milk can be dried up with increased exercise. If, however, your bitch is suffering with a false pregnancy and her nipples become hard and sore and mastitis is present, hormone injections should be administered by the vet. If you are uncertain, seek advice from your vet.

after her first litter, one is enough. Some bitches have a difficult whelping or are not sufficiently maternal by nature, and that should be taken into consideration before planning another litter.

During her season a bitch can be mated with a stud dog. There are two stages of the season: pro-oestrus and oestrus. Each stage lasts around nine days but the season in total lasts around three weeks. As your bitch comes into the pro-oestrus stage of the season she may urinate more, and the vulva will swell and leak a bloodstained discharge. During this stage she will attract a lot of male attention but will not be ready for mating. During the oestrus stage the vulva will enlarge further still but the discharge becomes a lighter, pinker colour. It is important to keep your Golden on the lead when out on walks during her season as she will attract lots of male attention and you do not want her to have an accidental pregnancy with the neighbour's dog. You may decide that for ease and security your bitch is best confined to the house and garden only during

*Only a few days old.*

the three weeks of her season. It is not necessary to change her feeding regime during this time. She may, however, require a bit of understanding from you, as the owner, as some Goldens go through slight behavioural changes during this time and can become more clingy and needy or, at the other end of the spectrum, irritable.

Your bitch will be most fertile at around eleven to fourteen days from the start of the season, during ovulation. It is at around this stage that she should be mated with a stud dog. If you are uncertain when your bitch is at the optimum time, a blood test can be carried out by the vet which will give a clear indication of when she is at her most fertile. You should have a suitable stud dog lined up before your bitch comes into season.

## THE STUD DOG

Choosing a suitable stud dog is very important. Simply choosing a dog that lives near you or is cheap to mate with is not acceptable. The stud dog must complement your bitch, depending on what type of offspring you are hoping for. For instance, if you have a Golden with a darker, wavy coat, and you want to continue that coat type in her puppies, do not choose a stud dog with a light cream coat. As a breeder, you should aim to produce puppies that are of excellent quality, both in type and temperament; sharing characteristics that both the bitch and the stud dog should have. As the owner of the bitch, you will be expected to visit the stud dog, and it is important to do so. You cannot gauge a dog, his temperament or his physical appearance by photos alone.

The first step is to research Golden Retriever stud dogs. Once you have made up a short list of potential stud dogs, you should contact the owners. Many stud dog owners will want to know about your bitch's pedigree and see photos of her before deciding whether to allow their stud dog to be used; some may also want to see her in person. The same care should be taken when selecting a stud dog to ensure he is healthy and of the correct type and temperament. Find out about his breeding, and ask as many questions as you can about him. Here are just a few questions you must ask:

### Is he Kennel Club registered?

If you are intending to register your litter with the Kennel Club, the stud dog must also be registered and in the correct ownership.

### Has he been health tested and what were the results?

The answer to this question must be yes. The stud dog should have had all the relevant tests done and his scores examined before deciding to mate him with your bitch. If his hip score is very high, he will likely pass this on to any progeny. Ask to see all his health test results and check that he has annual eye tests to ensure he is fit and healthy.

### Are there any endorsements restricting the registration of his progeny?

Any breeding restrictions placed on the stud dog will prevent the registration of the puppies, so it is important to find this out before mating.

### Has he produced any litters before?

A proven stud dog who is known to produce excellent puppies with good temperaments and free from hereditary diseases has many benefits over an unproven stud dog. However, every dog has to father his first litter, so if there is a potential stud dog that you particularly like you can ask for him. If the stud dog's owner is experienced, they may have a reserve stud dog just in case a mating does not take place with the chosen dog.

*OPPOSITE: The stud dog should complement your bitch and enhance her breeding potential.*

### How many litters has he currently sired?

The number of litters a stud dog has sired is important. A small number of litters proves he is an effective stud dog, but too many litters may be an indication that his owner is out to make money rather than selecting suitable bitches. Some stud dogs are known to have sired more than a hundred litters! Such over-use of a stud dog decreases the Golden Retriever gene pool and often leads to in-breeding.

### Are there any other possible matings he will have in the same period?

Make sure another bitch owner is not trying to use the same stud dog at the same time. A stud dog needs to be on top form to carry out a mating and he will not perform if he is exhausted.

### Is he a show dog, a working dog or a family pet?

If you intend to show or work any of the puppies, you will need to choose a suitable stud dog with the correct lineage for that type of activity. There is little point breeding a working bitch with a show-type stud dog and hoping for a field trial champion. That's not to say it doesn't happen occasionally but a proven type is a far safer option for optimum results.

### What is the stud fee?

The fee for a stud dog varies according to the type of dog chosen, and many factors can influence his price, including whether he is a champion of the show ring or field, and whether he has produced successful litters in the past or produced any puppies that have gone on to become winners in any activity. The average price for a stud dog is the fee of a puppy, so roughly £500–£700 and around £1,000 for champions. Some stud dog owners may wish to have first pick of the puppies in the litter if they want to keep one for themselves. You must be prepared to pay the stud dog fee whether your bitch falls pregnant or not, so choosing a stud dog who has never mated before to use on a maiden bitch is something of a gamble.

## THE MATING

Before the mating, your bitch should be in good condition and at her correct weight. There is no need to feed anything extra during the run-up to a mating and sometimes excess vitamins and minerals can be counterproductive. If you are unsure about the condition of your bitch, seek advice from your vet; a health check before mating is always advisable.

When your bitch is ready for mating (around eleven days into her season), you will have to take her to the

---

**Top Tip**

Checklist for breeding:

- Decide why you want to breed.
- Ask yourself whether you are suitable to breed; do you have enough time to dedicate to the puppies and have you done enough research.
- Decide what kind of breeder you want to be: an Assured Breeder, a regular breeder or a hobby breeder.
- Ensure that you have carried out all the health tests on your Golden and that the results are acceptable.
- Ensure that your Golden is of the correct sound temperament before deciding to breed.
- Select a suitable stud dog who meets all the requirements and complements your bitch both physically and in temperament.
- Plan the mating according to your bitch's seasons and a suitable time.
- Carry out another vet check to ensure your bitch is in top condition before mating.

stud dog. Normally, there will be two matings with the stud dog at least twenty-four hours apart (covering the eleven-to-fourteen-day fertile period). With an experienced stud dog, mating can happen quite quickly, but with dogs that are new to the game it can take hours for a successful mating. Generally not much human intervention is required, but a little direction doesn't go amiss if it appears that either the stud dog or the bitch is struggling.

The stud dog will be very excited when he first comes into contact with a bitch in season, and will sniff and lick around her vulva before attempting to mount her. The bitch will stand firmly with her tail held to one side. During mounting, the glands behind the penis will swell considerably and the vulva restricts, forcing the dog and bitch into a 'tie'. It is in this stage that they appear stuck together and the stud dog may want to dismount for comfort, in which case one of his hind legs can be lifted over the bitch and they can be turned rear end to rear end; the tie will still be secure and both dog and bitch comfortable. During this tie the semen will be ejaculated. If your bitch tries to move away or break free, hold on to her to stop her from causing any damage to herself or the dog. The tie can last anywhere from fifteen to forty minutes, and sometimes even longer, but at no time should anyone try to separate them. They will break free naturally when the glands have reduced in size. It is completely normal for some seminal fluid to drain from the vulva and does not mean the bitch is not pregnant.

After mating, you can leave your bitch to her own devices, though it is advisable not to let her run around too much straight after mating. If you have travelled to the stud dog owner, let your bitch have a drink and a bite to eat before taking her home again. You can then mate her again with the stud dog twenty-four to forty-eight hours later; there is no hard and fast rule on the second mating and it can take place up to three days after the first mating, depending on which day in her season the first mating took place. When both matings have taken place, ask the stud dog owner to sign the litter form (if you are registering your litter on a paper form) and complete all the registration details of the stud dog. If you are intending to register the litter online, you only require the dog's registration details.

## PREGNANCY

Three weeks after the mating you can take your bitch to your vet to confirm pregnancy. The vet may perform ultrasound imaging, just as for a human baby. There are also blood tests that measure the levels of the relaxin hormone. There is something quite exciting about seeing puppies on an ultrasound image, and you will also be able see roughly how many puppies to expect in the litter. You can also listen to the puppies' heartbeats using a stethoscope.

Your bitch's weight will increase during pregnancy and a change in body shape will be noticeable after day 50. Her nipples will also enlarge and it is not uncommon for her to start weeping milk a few days before whelping. The duration of pregnancy is normally sixty-three days, but can be as early as fifty-eight or as late as sixty-eight. In rare circumstances puppies have even been born before and after these dates but the average is around sixty-three days.

If your bitch was in peak condition prior to mating, she should continue on her normal feeding programme during the first few weeks of pregnancy and can be exercised daily as most foetuses develop fully in the last three to four weeks of pregnancy. There is a common misconception that a pregnant bitch should be over-fed and wrapped in cotton wool during the gestation, whereas in fact she should continue with her normal routine as much as possible, with the exception that she doesn't play rough games. She may have regular shorter walks right up until the whelping date, but allow her to move at her own pace. She can be brushed and bathed as normal during the early stages of pregnancy, but during the later stages just brushing is sufficient.

In the early weeks of pregnancy you do not need to feed her anything extra but during the final month you need to increase the amount of food given so she is receiving at least 50 per cent more food than she was on before mating. As Goldens are big food lovers, she will not require much encouragement to eat the extra food, but if you find she is becoming fussy give her smaller meals throughout the day. Again, you do not need to add in any other minerals, vitamins or calcium supplement; her normal balanced diet is all she requires.

*A bitch in the last days of pregnancy.*

Health is important during pregnancy and your bitch should continue the routine medication of worming and vaccinations. Consult with your vet regarding worming as she will require worming while pregnant and after whelping, which will protect the puppies from these parasites through her uterus and milk. Flea treatments can be used in the first stage of pregnancy but are not recommended again until the puppies are at least three weeks old.

Before the expected whelping date, you should set aside an area for her to have the puppies in. You may by now have an idea of how many puppies to expect, and how much space will be required. All puppies need space, and having twelve puppies is very different from having four puppies. The space needs to be large enough to fit a whelping box with enough room around it for the bitch to have a break. As the puppies start to walk, they will require a lot more room and space in the garden to run around. If you decide to raise the puppies

in a kennel, it needs to be warm and comfortable and regularly checked for cleanliness. There are pros and cons to raising puppies in a kennel: it is easy to clean and provides better ventilation, but can be damaging to the puppies' socialization and habituation. Also, puppies are more likely to be accidentally squashed by their mother if they are out of sight in a kennel than if someone is constantly with them. If space in the house is limited, or you are breeding regularly or have working Goldens who will most likely spend their life outside, then kennelling is preferable for obvious reasons.

For many others, though, raising puppies in the home is the ideal situation. Bear in mind that they will not be house-trained, so you may want to section off an area in the house with suitable flooring, such as a kitchen or utility room. If you have a very busy household or children, utility rooms make an excellent choice during the first few weeks of the puppies' life as it is quieter and away from distractions. Your bitch will want some

*A suitable whelping box should allow the bitch enough room to lie down both diagonally and horizontally.*

peace and quiet during those first few weeks to tend to her pups without being overly disturbed. Kitchens make an ideal room to raise the puppies as they grow. They are normally a suitable temperature, are easier to clean than, say, a lounge, and are the hub of the home where most of the daily activities take place, which is great for socialization and habituation. Whether you keep the litter inside or outside, the whelping area and surfaces should be cleaned regularly with disinfectant to minimize the spread of viruses, bacteria and odour.

As the whelping date looms, you need to prepare for the arrival of the puppies. The first thing to do is to set up a whelping box, which is a specifically designed box suitable for your bitch to give birth in and rear her

puppies. It will have four sides, one of which has a lowered ridge for access in and out of the box. There will also be bars or shelves around the sides; these are for the protection of the puppies as they prevent the bitch from accidentally lying on her pups. It can be made of cardboard (and thrown away after use), wood or plastic and should be large enough for your bitch to lie down in and to accommodate puppies until they are around four to five weeks old.

Your bitch needs to become accustomed to the whelping box, so it is a good idea to start placing comfortable bedding in there and encourage her to sleep in the box rather than in her bed. Provide suitable bedding: vet bed (a synthetic bedding material) is an excellent choice as it is warm, provides grip for the pups, allows fluids to soak through and can be washed easily. Place newspaper underneath the vet bed to soak up any fluids that seep through, and change the bedding and newspapers at least twice a day.

Heating is vital as puppies cannot regulate their body temperature during the first few weeks. There are heat mats (with washable covers) that can be placed underneath bedding to provide contact heat, and heat lamps that can be hung over the whelping box. Some purpose-built whelping boxes have a heated floor.

Puppies should be in a temperature of around 24 °C. The heat pad should be on during whelping as you will need to move the puppies to one side while your bitch continues to give birth.

Lighting should be subdued during the first two weeks as the pups begin to open their eyes. A side lamp is suitable as it is not as bright as main overhead lighting.

Whelping can take up to twenty-four hours, so make sure you have somewhere comfortable to sit and wait. Prepare a pile of clean towels: you will need plenty of

*As seen here, vet bed is a suitable bedding material. Keep a thermometer in the whelping box to ensure the temperature is correct.*

them to place underneath your bitch and to dry off the puppies.

Keep a notepad and pen handy to record the time of birth of each puppy. This is important as the intervals between puppies will be a clue to whether your bitch is struggling. As a guide, one puppy should be born each hour.

You will also need a set of scales to weigh the puppies at birth (and you should continue to monitor their weight until they go to a new home); and a vial, which can be used to assist breathing if a puppy's airway is blocked. Always have your vet's phone number to hand in case you need to call in an emergency. Do tell them in advance when the litter is due so they can also be prepared.

When your bitch is scanned, the vet will be able to give you a date on which you can expect the puppies. As the date comes closer, it is important to be with your dog at all times so you can be on hand in case complications arise. One indication that whelping will soon happen is your bitch's behaviour. She will become restless, refuse food and start nest building; her temperature drops and her vulva becomes swollen. At this stage encourage her to the whelping box, where she should give birth.

## WHELPING

The first stage of labour can last several hours. Your bitch will become incredibly restless, shiver and pant excessively as her cervix relaxes and dilates. Some bitches may also whine as a reaction to the pain. It is important to remember that giving birth is a natural process and the best way to help your bitch is to remain by her side and stay calm.

As she moves on to the second stage of labour she will frequently lick her vulva and you may see some abdominal straining. She will begin to lie down on her side at this stage, although some bitches prefer to give birth standing up. As tempting as it is to want to involve the entire family during the whelping process, note that the fewer people there are, the more comfortable your bitch will be. It is important she is calm and relaxed, and children can often be loud and excitable.

During this stage you will see strong abdominal strain-ing and a green-stained discharge. Straining can last around an hour, but if a puppy has not been produced after that time, seek veterinary help immediately as your bitch will tire and the puppies' lives could be at risk. Likewise, if the green-stained discharge increases and darkens, veterinary attention must be sought.

Puppies can be born with the membranes intact, in a sac full of fluid. The bitch will normally break the sac apart and eat it, tearing the umbilical cord herself. She will lick the puppy, which will clear his airway and stimulate him, and you will start to see movement and perhaps hear a few cries. You will know then that she has been successful. If she does not break the membrane, you must do so yourself with your nails and quickly clear the puppy's nose and mouth of any fluid. Using a cloth, clean up the puppy by rubbing it firmly between your hands. The umbilical cord will need to be torn, leaving about two inches left attached to the puppy. Under no circumstances must the cord be cut with scissors or pulled against the puppy's abdomen. Instead, hold it between your hands and rip it apart before discarding it. Place the puppy back on the bed, and if your bitch will settle down you can guide the puppy to a teat to suckle. If she is still restless, place the puppy in a warm box as she may be preparing for the next delivery.

Puppies can be born with the sac already ruptured, in which case you will be able to see the puppy's head or feet. It is perfectly normal, but your bitch may need a little help to deliver if she cannot expel the puppy herself. Very gently, pull the puppy in a downwards motion (away from the bitch's spine) in time with her straining. Newborn puppies are slippery, so you may need to hold on with a small piece of towelling. If a puppy is born with the membrane already ruptured, it will be normally be subsequently expelled. If there is no sign of a delivery, do not attempt to present a puppy yourself; assistance should only be given when a puppy is half-delivered.

After the first puppy is produced, subsequent puppies should appear after no more than thirty minutes of straining. Make a note of the time each puppy was born, its gender, and any distinguishing features. Offer your bitch a drink and a chance to relieve herself outside between puppies. Some bitches become instantly

*The umbilical cord that can be seen here will fall off after a couple of days and should not be pulled off.*

protective of their young and do not want to leave the box. This is perfectly normal, but if your bitch has not relieved herself for several hours, you can encourage her to come outside with you by carefully wrapping up a puppy to keep him warm and carrying him outside. Moving about can also encourage the next delivery, so take her outside if she has been straining for half an hour or so but no puppy has arrived.

Hours passing between puppies is abnormal and you should seek veterinary attention. There are numerous reasons for a lack of delivery. The puppies may be over-sized or in the wrong position, and it may be necessary for a caesarean section to be carried out. Your bitch should be taken to the veterinary practice immediately. If some puppies have already been born, keep them warm on the heated pad and have someone stay with them. If there is no one to stay with the puppies, you must bring them with you to the vet. Your bitch will be anaesthetized and woken up as soon as

all her puppies have been delivered. She will be able to go home within a few hours and will be able to nurse her litter normally. Her wound should, however, be kept clean and dry, and your vet will give you advice for her aftercare.

As each puppy is born, allow him the chance to suckle within the first hour of being born and dry him gently with a towel. They will sleep at some point during the whelping as it can take up to twenty-four hours for large litters. As your bitch contracts to produce another puppy, move the other puppies away and onto a heated pad to allow your bitch room to take care of the next puppy.

Once all the puppies are born, your bitch will relax and start to nurse her pups. Offer her some food to eat, but if she is comfortable do not force her. Once she is relaxed, she will probably fall asleep, which gives you time to examine the puppies. Ensure they are all dry and suckling happily and that none of them has any

*An exhausted bitch during whelping.*

obvious deformities. Check the temperature of the room and make sure the heat pad is working. At this stage there is no need to do anything else other than praise your girl, clean up and have a well-deserved celebratory drink (or sleep). It is advised that the bitch should be examined by your vet within twenty-four hours of whelping to ensure there are no puppies left inside. It is best to leave the puppies at home and take their mother after they have all had a feed and are contentedly sleeping. It is normal for the green discharge to continue for about twenty-four hours after whelping, and for the bloodstained discharge to continue for a few days and sometimes even for a couple of weeks, but any longer than that, especially if it is black and foul-smelling, veterinary advice should be sought.

## PUPPIES: UP TO TWO WEEKS OLD

The first two weeks will predominantly consist of watching over your bitch and her puppies. In the first two weeks puppies are like little slugs; they are unable to hear or open their eyes, and they spend most of their time feeding and sleeping. If any puppy is not feeding happily or putting on weight, speak to your vet as there may be an underlying problem. In the first two weeks the new mother will be preoccupied with them so make sure she is eating and drinking well and happily nursing her puppies. Some bitches will clean up after their puppies but the bedding should still be cleaned at least twice a day as urine will seep through the bedding and onto the box below (which, if it's cardboard, will shorten its lifespan). A newborn litter should not be left at home alone, so make sure there is always someone on hand to watch over them during the vital first two weeks. Some breeders even go to the length of sleeping next to the whelping box for the first two weeks to make sure the bitch does not accidentally lie on any of the puppies, which can lead to a distressing death. It is also vital that the puppies are kept warm during this time as hypothermia is a common cause of deaths in young puppies.

The puppies should be weighed on a daily basis to check they are growing progressively. Any small or weak puppies can be fed puppy milk, which can be obtained from pet shops, to supplement their mother's milk. Puppy milk can also be useful if your bitch has a large litter and is overwhelmed by more puppies than she has teats.

Increase your bitch's feeding programme once she has had her puppies. A nursing bitch will lose a lot of condition, putting all her energy into feeding her young. To ensure she produces enough milk to provide for all her puppies and maintains good condition, her food must be gradually increased during the four weeks before the expected whelping date, and once the litter is born she should be eating up to four times more than her normal amount. There are specially formulated complete feeds suitable for nursing bitches, and a good pet store will be able to advise on the most suitable product. A few leftovers that are high in protein, such as eggs, fish and chicken, are fine to give her. While she is rearing a litter, it is more advisable to feed your bitch a complete dog mix rather than a raw diet as all the supplements needed for a healthy litter will be incorporated and puppies may suffer from malnourishment if they do not receive the correct nutrition.

*Newborn puppies will often huddle together for warmth.*

Check your bitch's nipples on a daily basis for any hardness, heat or cracking of the teats. You should be able to express a small amount of milk but if the teats are swollen or are not producing milk, or there is blood in the milk, she may have mastitis. If you suspect mastitis, consult your vet. If you do not, the condition may worsen, which will lead to her being unable to produce milk and you will have to hand-feed the puppies until they are on solid food.

For the first two weeks puppies should be indoors, somewhere quiet, dark and away from the busy household, such as in a utility room or cloakroom. As they reach three to four weeks old they can be moved.

## PUPPIES: THREE TO SIX WEEKS OLD

During this period puppies start to explore their world, and become far more mobile, inquisitive and fun. They are at their most demanding at this age and there will be a lot of cleaning up to do.

At this age the puppies may be moved outside into a suitable enclosed kennel, which is draught-free, well heated and offers comfortable bedding, as well as access to an outside space. If you are raising a litter in a kennel or purpose-built shed, the following three things are vital:

- The puppies must be kept warm; they are still susceptible to hypothermia at this age;
- The puppies must receive daily social contact with handling;
- The puppies must be properly exposed to the household lifestyle; taking them out of the kennel to run around the garden and areas such as the kitchen will help to prepare them for their future homes.

*At around three to four weeks old puppies will become very curious and begin to venture beyond the whelping box.*

*If the weather is nice the puppies can play outside. Here a mat has been placed on top of the decking to prevent small paws slipping down the gaps.*

If you are a hobby breeder, moving the litter to an area such as the kitchen is probably easiest for you, your bitch and her puppies. If the kitchen is not suitable, any large area where the puppies can move around freely will be adequate. If you have a large enough area, it is a good idea to enclose half of it to make a playpen, so they can run around safely and are not restricted to the whelping box. Being brought up in the house allows the puppies to experience normal daily activities and to hear and see everything that is going on. It also provides peace of mind for the breeder as you will be able to keep a close eye on them to ensure they do not come to any harm. More often than not, raising puppies in the home means they will be handled more regularly, their play and bedding areas will be more hygienic as you will be able to clean them up as soon as they are soiled, and your bitch will be in her own environment.

Encourage young pups to toilet away from their bed by laying down newspaper and praising them when they toilet there, just as you would any young puppy in your home. The only difference is, rather than having one puppy to praise, you may have twelve. Raising puppies like this also has the benefit that new owners will be impressed that their puppy has some basic house manners and is already used to living in a home.

## PUPPIES: SIX TO EIGHT WEEKS OLD

At this stage the puppies start to develop individual characters, interact with everything around them and require a lot of stimulation. They will be inquisitive and into everything, climbing on everything and chewing everything. It is their way of distinguishing what is around them. It is also a time to keep a careful eye on them to make sure they are not chewing anything dangerous or causing too much mischief. Mostly they will be interested in playing with their litter mates but it is a vital time to start the learning process of going to a new home.

The puppies should be handled every day away from

*Puppies should be played with every day and by different people in the household so they become accustomed to being handled.*

**Top Tip**

Checklist on whelping:

- Prepare for mating; if you are unsure of the best day for mating, blood tests can be carried out by your vet.
- Mating between bitch and stud, followed by second mating.
- Ensure your bitch is looked after as normal during the early stages of pregnancy.
- Have a pregnancy scan carried out.
- Increase your bitch's food intake during the last four weeks of pregnancy.
- Decrease your bitch's exercise regime.
- Set up the whelping box and begin encouraging your bitch to sleep in it.
- Prepare for whelping.
- Keep your vet's contact details to hand during whelping.
- Be prepared for whelping to take up to twenty-four hours; try to prepare for all possible outcomes.
- Keep the whelping box clean during the first couple of weeks and allow mum to nurse her new-borns.
- Always clean up after puppies straight away.
- The puppies will start to explore their world.
- Look after mum and let her rest.
- Begin weaning the puppies off milk and onto soaked puppy food, and then progress to harder puppy food.
- Begin the socialization, habituation and basic training of puppies.

the litter and played with so they begin to bond with people. Puppies who play only with their litter mates and only have human interaction when it is required will struggle when they come to be rehomed. If you can begin the process of interacting with them before they go to their new homes it will assist their developing independence. Puppies will naturally want to play with anyone, so encouraging them to interact with you is not difficult.

## PUPPIES: FEEDING

You can use a complete puppy food soaked in water to make it easier for the puppies to eat. You can also introduce chopped beef, scrambled eggs and cooked chicken for protein and fat. It is not advisable to offer puppies cereals such as Weetabix with milk. It used to be a popular option among breeders, but it has been proven that dogs are lactose-intolerant and they should not have skimmed cow's milk. If you want to give your puppies some dairy, which is perfectly acceptable, offer them goat's milk or natural yoghurt. Home-made diets made up purely of cereals and meat will not supply the puppies with all their nutritional needs and in these first few weeks it is vital they get all the nutrients they need to grow and develop.

At this age the puppies will probably still be feeding from their mum and puppy food should be provided in small quantities to wean them off gently. When you give them their puppy food, separate your bitch from them; that way she can get some much-needed rest and it will allow her milk to start drying up. Some bitches will quite happily carry on feeding their puppies until they are ready to leave for their new homes, but weaning them before they leave allows them to adapt to their new food source. Each bitch and each litter is different and you will be able to judge whether your bitch is happy to feed them or whether she needs space, and whether the pups are putting on weight correctly or not eating enough, and you can portion

*Wean puppies on to a wet mix before starting real solid food.*

### Top Tip

- When feeding puppies, bear in mind that they require more food relative to their weight than adults do.
- Puppies have very small stomachs so need feeding regularly throughout the day.
- For growth, puppies require a good quality, easily digestible and high protein diet.
- Puppies can still be allowed to nurse from their mother once they are eating solid food, as long as she allows it. But from a weaning perspective, if they are still nursing from mum your puppies may suffer far more separation anxiety when they go to their new homes, so it is kinder to wean them from their mother before they go.
- Cow's milk contains too little protein, fat, calcium and energy to be a substitute for the bitch's milk.
- Evaporated milk contains too much lactose, which can cause severe diarrhoea.

*Puppies can be given individual or collective bowls; here, a piece of guttering has been neatly turned into a feed trough.*

food out accordingly. Puppy food should be soaked while the puppies are being weaned as they will not be used to solid foods. Over a period of a few weeks you can start introducing more solid foods. As puppies eat their bellies expand and become large and round, which is normal and healthy and ideal. Feeding time can get very messy as puppies will step in their food, lie in their food, sit in it and play with it. Ideally, place the food in a shallow bowl away their bedding area, with plenty of newspaper around it and allow them to eat happily. If there are some puppies who are struggling to get to the food, try putting down several bowls so everyone gets a fair amount. Some pups may need

encouragement to eat from a bowl; start by feeding from your hand and then placing it in the bowl. Once they have finished eating, pick up all the bowls as otherwise they will become play toys or may be toileted on. Continue to wean the puppies off their mother's milk gradually so that by the time they are six to seven weeks old they are eating independently and on four or five good meals a day. It is worth writing down for new owners what food the puppies are on, how much they are fed and how often. It is also helpful to provide new owners with a little bag of the puppy food for them to take away to get them started for the first few days.

## PUPPIES: REGISTERING AND ADVERTISING

Once your puppies are registered with the Kennel Club (KC), you are eligible to advertise on their website. Puppies can be registered as soon as they are born, but it is worth waiting a couple of weeks at least to ensure all the puppies are fit and healthy. Registering your litter can be done online or on paper on a Kennel Club litter form.

If you want to have a kennel name, you will need to apply for it months before the litter is born as registration is often a lengthy process and name options can be limited. The kennel name must be unique to you, and not similar to any other registered kennel name in use.

The kennel name is used as a prefix at the beginning of each puppy's name. It is their identity tag to show their bloodlines and links to a breeder. You do not need a kennel name to register a litter, but naming puppies can more difficult without one as puppy names cannot be duplicated within the same breed. For instance, a name such as Golden Blossom will be more than likely be registered already. Puppy names must have at least one word. If all your name choices are not available, for a small fee you can use the Kennel Club's annual kennel name.

It is during registration that you, as the breeder, can decide whether to place any endorsements on your puppies to enforce breeding and export restrictions. Once registered, each puppy will be given a registration form, which lists his name, registration number, breed, date of birth, parentage, colour, sex and any endorsements. If you wish, you will also receive a five-

*Be careful where you advertise your puppies.*

generation pedigree certificate showing the puppy's family tree. This documentation should be signed by the breeder(s) and handed to the new owners when they collect the puppy.

When your puppies are around six weeks old, you may want to start advertising them further afield. Where once puppies were advertised in local newspaper and shop windows, the majority of breeders now advertise on the internet. If you own a kennel name and breed regularly, having your own website can be beneficial as it constantly advertises your bloodlines whether you have a litter available or not. This type of advertising often leads to waiting lists, where new owners choose to wait for one of your puppies rather than go elsewhere. There are numerous websites that advertise puppies for sale, but you should only advertise on reputable websites to target the most suitable new homes.

## PUPPIES: PROSPECTIVE OWNERS

Once the puppies are four weeks old, allow prospective owners to come and view them. (Visits when they are younger than four weeks could make the puppies susceptible to illness and stress; moreover, since puppies don't develop their distinct characters until this age, the owner won't really be able to see what their puppy is like.) Prospective owners will ring and ask lots of questions, and you in turn should also ask lots of questions before allowing them to visit the puppies. Some initial questions worth asking are:

- Why do you want a puppy?
- Why do you want a Golden Retriever?
- Why do you want one of my puppies in particular?
- What are you looking for in a puppy – for instance, do you want a puppy for working in the field, showing, any other activities or as a pet?
- Do you live in a town or in the countryside?
- Do you live in a house suitable for dogs?
- Do you have a large garden?
- Are you prepared to walk your Golden every day in every type of weather?
- How many people live in the household? Do you have any children? (Goldens make exceptional puppies for children, but if the children are very

*Always encourage new owners to visit the puppies a couple of times before picking their puppy.*

small, a big boisterous dog may not be suitable and new parents may find juggling a puppy and children difficult.)

- Have you owned a Golden Retriever before?
- Have you researched Golden Retrievers?
- Do you work full-time?
- What will happen to the puppy during the day?
- Do you want a girl or a boy?
- What colouring are you looking for? (Some owners will have a strong preference. If you have bred a cream litter, and the owners want a dark golden, it is best to say no, as the puppies should go to a home where they are wanted 100 per cent exactly as they are.)

It is worth pointing out all the traits of Golden Retrievers at this stage as it is amazing how many new owners pick a puppy because it is cute, rather than researching about the breed and what to expect.

If you are unhappy with any of the answers the prospective owners give, be prepared to be strong enough to say no to them. It is far better to say no over the phone than to allow someone to meet the puppies, fall in love with one and then refuse. If you are uncertain, err on the side of caution and do not let the prospective owner visit. Good breeders will want to see their puppies go to the very best homes.

If you are happy to let the prospective owners come and visit, suggest a suitable time when they can come over. Bear in mind that most people will want to visit in the evenings and at weekends. When they come, allow them to see the puppies with their mum and in their area, rather than bringing puppies out to be seen. If possible, try to arrange visits for times when you know the puppies will be awake (so not straight after a feed or too late in the evening). Avoid booking up too many visits in one day, as back-to-back visits can be exhausting, not only for you but also for your bitch and the puppies.

Allow the prospective owners to spend some time with the litter and play with them. Normally it is during this time that they will confirm whether they would like one of your puppies, and you can decide if you would like them to have one. Some prospective owners may want to pick a puppy on the first visit, and it really is up to the breeder whether you allow this or encourage them to make a second visit before choosing.

As a breeder myself, I always encourage prospective owners to come twice before picking a puppy to make sure they have chosen correctly. If the new owners have visited the puppies when they are particularly quiet, it will give a false impression of their characters. And if they have picked a puppy with lots of character who happens to be quiet when they visit, this should also be mentioned to them. They may reserve a puppy of their choice but they should 'sleep on it' before making a definite decision.

It is worth asking for a deposit when owners have chosen their puppy; this ensures no messing around from either party and confirms the sale. The deposit amount varies from breeder to breeder, but the recommended amount is normally £100.

The prospective owners should ask more questions when they meet the litter, and this is a good time to ask any other questions you may have about them and their expectations. You may want to talk about any training the puppies have already had, their routine, their diet, their worming regime, and whether they will be vaccinated and microchipped before they leave. This is also the ideal time to mention registration of the puppies, and any endorsements and other conditions you may want to put in your contract.

Some new owners will want to come and visit their puppy many times before they take him or her home, and this is the ideal situation. It allows the puppy to recognize his new owner and start to build a bond, making the separation far easier when the time comes for him to go to his new home. The new owners should also bring over an item of clothing or bedding that can be put in with the litter and then taken home with them when they collect their puppy. Because it will smell of the litter, it can provide some comfort for the puppy leaving the nest.

If the new owner is unable to visit again because of distance or other commitments, stay in touch with them, sending pictures and providing updates. It will help to build a connection between the new owner and the puppy and will satisfy the eager new owner.

During the interval between the first visit and collecting the puppy, the new owners should be preparing

*Here the breeder has a plush toy for each puppy to take to their new home that smells of the litter.*

for the arrival, and they may be in regular contact and asking for lots of advice. As the breeder, you should give them as much information as you can. It will be an exciting time for the new owner and the chances are they will not take all the information in, so providing a puppy pack gives them something to go to if they are uncertain. The puppy pack should be given to the new owners on the day they collect the puppy. It should cover a variety of information, such as feeding, exercise, daily routine, veterinary information, dates of flea and worm treatment, microchipping details and paperwork, four weeks' free insurance, the Kennel Club registration papers for the puppy and the signed transfer of ownership, the contract and anything else required. You may decide to buy each

puppy a collar; not only will it get the puppies used to wearing them, but is a nice token to send the puppy away with.

## REARING AT ITS BEST

As the breeder, you play an important role in the first stage of a puppy's life, so it is incumbent upon you to do your very best. You will only have a window of about four weeks during which to implement some socialization, habituation and training. It is up to you to start this process so the puppies have the best possible start in life, where they are cared for, looked after properly and can establish some level of 'normal living'. Even working dogs who are bred outside, and will spend

*Puppies are interested in and have to 'touch' absolutely everything.*

their lives outside, require the same sort of socialization; only their habituation will be different. They may need to be accustomed to different situations and experience other noises before they go to their new home. It will be scary for a puppy who begins life in a quiet, purpose-built kennel to move to a busy farm where he will be exposed to a whole range of loud noises and unfamiliar situations.

Puppies who do not get the correct amount of interaction with the breeder, or who are not looked after appropriately, may end up either being returned to the breeder further down the line or being a disappointment to the new owners. To provide a level of habituation before the puppies go to their new homes, try to expose them to some or all of the following:

- Hoovers
- Dishwashers
- Washing machines
- Clattering of crockery and cutlery
- Telephone ringing
- Television
- Radio
- Conversations
- Children and adults
- Garden equipment, such as wheelbarrows, hose pipes and lawnmowers
- Food preparation. (Preparing and cooking food in front of young puppies means they are less inclined to get in the cook's way waiting for a morsel of food to fall on the floor.)

Although the majority of each puppy's training will be done in his new home, you can begin some level of basic commands, such as sit, and begin toilet training. To get a whole litter toilet trained is easier said than done, especially if you have a large litter, as you will not be able to watch them all. To begin the toilet training process, first thing in the morning take the entire litter out into the garden. If any of them do toilet outside, make a huge fuss of them and give them a little treat, which can just be a little of their food. Sometimes if one goes, the others will follow suit. Take them out regularly during the day, after they wake up and soon after they eat, regardless of the weather. They need to learn to toilet outside, even when it is raining. Let the puppies toilet anywhere they want outside: now is not the time to be selective over where they go! They will soon get into the habit of toileting outside, and it will make toilet training for the new owners much easier if the puppies

*As the puppies grow, there should be two compartments in the box: bedding and a toileting area.*

*Provide a variety of toys for the puppies to play with.*

are used to going out rather than being left to toilet in their bedding or play areas. You can also put newspaper down on the floor in the house to allow puppies to toilet on: it is easier to clean up and still begins the toilet training process.

Never let the puppies out in the garden unattended. Even the best prepared garden still has its dangers for a litter of young puppies, and if there is a gap in the fencing you had not spotted you can be sure they'll find it. Try not to be garden proud: if you have an enviable lawn or beautiful borders, it is all guaranteed to be squashed, chewed and toileted on or dug up. Remember that it is only for a short period of time and plants and lawns do grow back. If you have the space, you can fence off areas you do not want the puppies to go into.

You should be handling the puppies every day (which is not hard to do as they are irresistible). During handling, they should be weighed, their bodies checked all over and, ideally, their toenails clipped. It is very easy to clip a young puppy's toenails as they curve at the very end and you can, using your own nail, feel the point where they hook over. Using normal nail clippers (not the ones designed for dog use as they are too large for puppies), clip off the hook at the end of the nail, and then reward the puppy. This will get him used to having his nails clipped from an early age; this is something many new owners struggle with, and many people end up with an older dog who hates having his nails trimmed. Clipping the tip causes no pain at all, as you are taking off such a small amount it is nowhere near the quick. Clipping the nails takes off the sharpness and begins the grooming training process.

You can also begin to wipe feet with a towel: when the puppies come in from outside or are muddy, you can pat them dry and clean off their paws. They will undoubtedly have to be towelled down when they go to their new homes, so starting the process early does no harm; just don't expect any of the puppies to stay still. You can also bath the puppies, but their coats will contain natural oils that protect their coat and skin so I personally would not bath a young puppy unless it was really necessary.

Give the puppies plenty of stimulation. While they will happily play with their litter mates, once they leave they will be playing with toys, so provide them with a range of suitable toys that they can have fun with and interact with. You can also play with them and provide human interaction through play. Suitable puppy toys can be purchased at any good pet shop; buy a selection as any damaged toys must be thrown out straight away to ensure no small pieces are accidentally swallowed.

## THE PUPPY CONTRACT

Every puppy should be supplied with a sales contract. It is vital that you go through the contract with the new owners and have them sign two copies, so they can have a copy and you can keep one for yourself. The contract should cover the terms and conditions of the sale, the price, and what happens to the puppy should the new owner no longer be able to keep him.

The contract should be typed up and two copies printed out. It should contain details about the puppy (his registration name, registration number, breed, date of birth, colour and sex) and about you as the breeder (your name, address, telephone number, website and Assured Breeder status, if applicable). It should also contain a statement regarding the sale, along the lines of the following:

This contract confirms the sale of the above-described dog between the breeder (insert details) and the purchaser (insert details).

The breeder (insert name) has taken every care in the breeding, rearing, health and welfare of the above-mentioned dog and is sold to (insert name) in the belief that the dog is in good health (insert any veterinary confirmations about this), and the breeder makes no warranty as to the health of the dog. The parents of the above-mentioned dog have received the following health schemes (insert health test results) and the puppy has received the following health schemes (insert as applicable) to avoid the possibility of inherited diseases.

You should also include details on the terms of returning the dog. As a responsible breeder, you must be prepared to have any puppy returned to you at any stage in his life, and he can then be rehomed adequately if required. Payment terms will vary depending on the circumstance, but you can use the following wording for guidance:

'The purchaser (insert name) has X days to return the puppy to the breeder (insert name), whereby the purchaser (insert name) will be refunded the full purchase price on condition that the following aspects have been met: the puppy has not suffered any illness or injury while in the keeping of the purchaser which could be detrimental to the puppy; the puppy is being returned in good faith that he/she is in the same condition as when he/she left the breeder; ownership of the puppy has not been transferred nor the microchip details transferred into the purchaser's name; and all documentation belonging to the puppy must be returned to the breeder. Failure to comply with any of the above-mentioned conditions will result in a deduction from the refunded amount to the purchaser.

'The purchaser (insert name) must return the dog to the breeder (insert name) should they no longer desire

**Top Tip**

Checklist on rearing puppies:

- Ensure the puppies are getting the right quantity of food and are being weaned;
- Register the litter with the Kennel Club and place any endorsements;
- Advertise the litter;
- Interview prospective owners;
- Encourage new owners to visit their puppy more than once;
- Create a contract and puppy pack for new owners;
- Keep up with training, socialization and habituation for the puppies;
- Be ready to let them go to their new homes.

*Letting puppies go to their new homes can be difficult.*

or be able to keep the dog. The dog must not be placed into the care of any rescue or rehoming centre, nor rehomed or sold on by the purchaser. The dog may be returned at any age after the initial X days of initial purchase, at which point no refund will be provided. The breeder has full disclosure of the keeping of the dog, whether it is seen necessary to keep, rehome or sell the dog.

'The breeder cannot be held responsible for any distress caused by returning the dog.'

If you are selling a puppy to a home where the new owners wish to compete with their dog in showing, field trials, other activities or breeding, written details must be included regarding those expectations. The following can be used for guidance on the wording:

'No warranty can be given to the show/field trial (or any other activity) and/or breeding potential of the above-mentioned dog and the breeder cannot be held responsible for the outcome of the following: failure to

be placed at any level activity including showing and field trials; any health scheme results following health testing; unsuccessful mating. (List any other relevant details.)'

You must list any endorsements placed on the puppy, and any terms that will lead to the lifting of those endorsements. The following can be used for guidance on the wording:

'The above-mentioned dog is endorsed with the following endorsements: (list endorsements and their meaning). The endorsements may only be lifted by the person(s) who placed them in writing to the Kennel Club.

'The endorsements may be lifted, subject to meeting the following requirements: (list any requirements here; for example, under breeding restrictions you may specify that the puppy, at the right age, has all the necessary health tests done and that the test results are satisfactory before he is used for breeding, that

*The loveable look of a Golden puppy.*

the puppy is not bred from under the minimum age, and is not mated prior to the endorsements being lifted).

'The breeder reserves the right not to lift the endorsements should any of the above requirements not be met.'

In the final section you must specify the sale price of the puppy and the date. Both parties must sign the contract, and there should be a declaration for the purchaser to sign. The following can be used for guidance on the wording: 'I/we confirm that I/we have read and agree to the terms listed and outlined in this contract.'

It is vital that the contract is covered in detail with the new owners and they fully understand the terms. Ensure that both copies of the contract are signed and you retain one copy for your files in case of any disputes further down the line.

## PUPPIES: LEAVING THE NEST

At eight weeks old the puppies will be ready to go to their new homes. No puppy should leave the nest before eight weeks as it is detrimental to their well-being and development. Even if a new owner says they can only take their puppy home at a certain time, they will have to wait until he is eight weeks old at the very earliest.

When the puppies are ready to go, try to avoid letting them all go on the same day, as this will be very traumatic for the bitch. Aim to let one puppy go each day, as this allows the mother to accept that the puppies are going, will be easier for the puppies left behind and less heartbreaking for you.

Ensure you have everything ready before the new owners turn up. You will need:

- the puppy pack
- the Kennel Club registration
- a small piece of bedding for the owners to take with them
- a small bag of the puppy's food
- any items you are giving to the puppy; i.e. a collar, lead, toy, etc.

It is traumatic letting the puppies go: you have raised them and looked after them from the day they were born, and given them the best chance in life. But it is some comfort to know that, as the breeder, you have done your best and given each puppy the best start in life.

Many owners will contact the breeder in the first few weeks if they have any concerns or just to say how the puppy is doing. Many owners and breeders stay in contact with each other, which is reassuring for both parties: the breeder can see their puppy is happy and healthy, and the owner has someone they can turn to for advice and support. You may want to run gatherings each year to mark the puppies' birthday; it is a great way for the litter to meet up again and for owners to exchange stories and ask for help or advice.

One thing has brought you all together: your love for Golden Retrievers.

# CONCLUSION

The Golden Retriever continues to adapt to modern life. From its origins as a true working dog, being kept only by a few sportsmen in the late nineteenth century, through gaining popularity after appearing in the show ring in the early twentieth century with notable Golden enthusiasts such as Lewis (Loulou) Harcourt and Colonel William Le Poer Trench, the Golden Retriever went from working dog to show dog, and from these roots has gone on to become a great working and service dog and a perfect family pet, as well as still being a real competitor in the field and show ring.

The Golden Retriever is the friend who never criticizes, never tells secrets, never betrays and is always there, with a wagging tail and a happy heart; they are adaptable dogs, and their loyalty, their unconditional love and their friendship will see them through the next hundred years.

*A friend for life.*

# ACKNOWLEDGEMENTS

It's been what seems like a very long journey and I couldn't have done it without the following people and organizations.

I would like to thank Sue Dobson, Jan Howe and Susanna Zubair of Thornywait Golden Retrievers for the photographs of their beautiful dogs and their contribution; Hart Veterinary Centre for photographs and their expertise; Canine Partners; Dogs for the Disabled; Dogs Trust; Medical Dedication Dogs and The Kennel Club for their contributions, and I would like to say a special thanks to Anne King for her expertise, her beautiful dogs and her dedication.

I would also like to thank my family and friends for their help and support. And last, but not least, a special person who has helped me in so many ways to finish this book.

And, of course, to all Golden Retrievers!

# INDEX